'*A practical and inspiring guide to turning ideas into cash from a master of customer insight and innovation.*'

Tim Brown CEO of IDEO, the USA's most renowned design and innovation consultancy

---

'*Anyone with the ambition, determination and passion to build something great should read this book first – it unlocks the secret to financing ideas.*'

Nigel Grierson, managing director and co-founder of Doughty Hanson Technology Ventures (one of Europe's largest Venture Capital firms)

'*At Egg, Mike Harris and his small team of bright-eyed entrepreneurs set out to transform banking in the UK. That they did in spades, setting the standard for electronic banking worldwide.*'

Gordon Starr, founder of Starrco, San Francisco based experts in transformation of organizational culture.

'*All you need to know about customer engagement, leadership, innovation, and culture whether you are starting a new business or transforming an existing organization.*'

Peter Darbee, chairman and CEO of California energy Giant, Pacific Gas and Electric

---

'*Mike is one of the great serial entrepreneurs, having built three businesses with market valuations in excess of £1 billion. Mike has led many highly successful seminars at MIT that provoke students to think about the process for delivering breakthrough innovations. His descriptions of where innovations come from are brilliant.*'

Henry Birdseye Weil, senior lecturer, MIT Sloan School of Management

Find Your Lightbulb

How to make millions from apparently impossible ideas

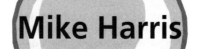

Mike Harris

CAPSTONE

Dedication

*For Sue, a light still burning brightly after all these years;
and all of my deeply loveable, highly entertaining
and perhaps just slightly eccentric close family.*

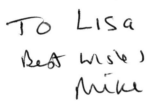

Contents

Acknowledgements

Firstly, I would like to thank my editor Lisa Murray for doing such a fantastic job in organizing the content of this book and re-expressing my thoughts in such an elegant fashion. She had the uncanny ability of unearthing the exact insights required from our interviews with entrepreneurs and innovators, as well as questioning every one of my words in a reassuringly forensic fashion.

As one entrepreneur (who shall remain nameless) commented to me after reading his extract: 'That woman is good!' She is good and, throughout the really tough process of writing a book – particularly a first book – I was more than grateful for her assistance.

I also want to thank all those busy people who gave up their precious time to contribute, and acknowledge them all for their continuing skill and commitment to making big ideas happen. In particular, Tom Ilube (CEO of Garlik), Peter Darbee (Chairman and CEO of Californian energy giant PG&E) and Richard Reed (co-founder of Innocent Drinks), who all allowed me to write in such detail about their leadership. I also owe a lot to Tracy Goss and Gordon Starr – they have taught me so much over the years about leadership, culture and business coaching.

In addition, I'd like to thank the leadership teams that worked for me at Firstdirect, Mercury and Egg – I'll always appreciate what they did.

And I couldn't get away without mentioning Thomas Edison, whose work inspired the title of this book and whose inventions (including the lightbulb) effectively ushered in the modern world.

And finally big, heartfelt thanks to Tim Berners-Lee, Bill Gates and Steve Jobs. Our current digital age is truly a perfect stage for the entrepreneur and the innovator, and I believe these three gentlemen effectively caused it to happen.

Introduction

This book is about beating the odds.

I truly believe that anyone with enough enthusiasm and determination can make millions out of nothing more than a simple idea.

The biggest problem most people face is not knowing how or where to start. Others are deterred in the first instance because they feel the odds of success are entirely stacked against them.

However, having built several valuable businesses in a row, I am absolutely confident that I can light the way and shift the odds dramatically in your favour.

In 2006, I was speaking to a group of young executives on a mid-career MBA course at the Sloan School of Management at MIT. I told them that I had spent the past 20 years turning new ideas into billion-dollar businesses. According to the experts, most of these ideas were impossible. When I explained that I could help anyone turn their business dreams into reality, it was as if lightbulbs were turning on all around the room.

Just thinking about creating something worthwhile and making money at the same time really turned them on – it turns everyone on. And thankfully, it's an opportunity available to anyone who wants to take it.

I consider myself a regular sort of person. While my success is definitely not a unique form of superhuman genius like Steve Jobs, Bill Gates or Richard Branson, I also refuse to believe that starting five successful businesses in a row has all been down to luck. I think my secret has been a willingness to learn from others coupled with a genuine interest in experimenting with different approaches to leadership and innovation.

Indeed, the past 20 years has taught me that many successful entrepreneurs struggled through their early periods hardly knowing what they were doing. Enthusiasm, a big vision and an unwillingness to be derailed by their critics got them through the tough times. That was certainly true of me at my first company, Firstdirect.

My experience has also shown me that early success for many companies often came about through a mixture of sheer determination and unexpected good luck. Once things took off, the founders had to scramble wildly to learn the basics of big business: customer insight, funding, strategy, brand, culture and leadership. An inability to do so often results in failure, just at the point where everything was starting to take shape.

For these reasons I have sought to give budding entrepreneurs:

- a step-by-step manual to assist you in getting started
- an early heads-up on all the aspects of business you will need to take care of in order to lead your company to sustainable success
- an easy and affordable way to use powerful leadership, planning and marketing techniques in the earliest days of your business

The principles I describe have been derived from my own direct experience, along with invaluable insights and words of wisdom from an army of entrepreneurs and innovators. Together we have been responsible for the successful implementation of new ideas in the fields of Internet, business and consumer software, business services, financial services, telecommunications, travel, manufacture of consumer goods, media, health, retailing, consumer services, energy, and technology.

I believe that a society rich in entrepreneurship and innovation benefits all of us. And so I invite you to unleash your own lightbulb, and discover your unique power to take an idea from anywhere and light up the world with your love and enthusiasm for it.

Are you ready to place your bet?

1

Living the dream

'In each of us there is a private hope and dream which, fulfilled,
can be translated into benefit for everyone.'

John F. Kennedy, 35th US President

———————

This book is for people who want to change their lives irrevocably by creating something valuable out of nothing more than a simple idea. There are many ways to make a living, but few are as satisfying as starting your own business and bringing something new into the world.

I've created three billion-pound businesses from scratch and been chairman of a fourth, which was sold for $10bn less than a decade after it started. I'm currently working on my fifth business creation and still enjoying every minute.

Have you ever dreamt that you might be able to do the same – make a million from unleashing your idea into the world? Or have you found excuses and listened to all those people who put you down?

Well, at the end of this chapter I'll tell you exactly what to do to start living your dream. But first let me tell you the most important things I've learned about making ideas happen – things that I firmly believe will motivate you into taking those first few steps.

> - Your own enthusiasm for an idea is what will bring it to life.
> - Everyone struggles to take the first bold step, but once you have, you will stop dreaming and start living.
> - You don't need to be superhuman to make a great and successful entrepreneur.
> - The expertise and genius of entrepreneurs is not in coming up with complex ideas – most of the time it's down to simple ideas fantastically well implemented.

Enthusiasm conquers all

In May 2002, I found myself arriving by boat at Bill Gates' residence. He was hosting the annual Microsoft dinner for the chief executives of its most important customers. Minutes later I was walking towards his magnificent 50,000 square foot mansion overlooking Lake Washington in Medina, near Seattle. I was full of excitement, mixed with nervous anticipation.

The Microsoft CEO summit is a serious event, with heavyweight presentations and panel discussions. Despite the networking necessities and obligatory small talk, I was actually really enjoying myself. I'd already had great fun with Jeff Bezos (founder of Amazon), tormenting the technicians by trying to get a prototype of Bill's new enthusiasm, the tablet PC, to work. It turned out the machine we were using was faulty. I had bumped into Warren Buffett, the second richest man in the world and something of a mentor to Bill. Warren asked me how long I'd been married. When I told him I thought it was about 30 years, he responded: 'You must have learned the secret of successful long-term relationships.' When I said not really, he walked away chuckling and turning back towards me muttered, 'Low expectations, that's the secret.'

Later I listened intently as Bill's wife Melinda explained how he was in charge of the network of 40 PCs that ran all of the digital features of their home. It's funny to imagine him doing what an IT administrator in a small company does, but equipping your house with 40 PCs definitely shows an enthusiasm for your own product.

I finally got to shake hands with Bill later that evening.

'Mike Harris, founder of Egg,' I said. 'We're an Internet bank, one of the first in the world and right now the biggest.'

'I know Egg,' Bill replied. 'I gave the keynote at a conference where one of your guys spoke last month.'

I went on to tell Bill that Egg and Microsoft had been working together for a while on some new ideas, and how we seemed to share something of a common philosophy.

The following year Bill was on a platform in front of thousands of people with Egg CIO Tom Ilube. He was demonstrating an Internet banking application that Egg and Microsoft had co-developed to show how emerging technologies such as Vista (Microsoft's then new operating system) could transform customers' experience of using the Web. Bill introduced Egg as 'simply the best example of implementing these new technologies'.

So how did a company such as Egg, which was tiny in comparison to other banks and should have been well under Gates' radar, get so much attention? And why was I able to claim Egg and Microsoft seemed to have something of a common philosophy? And what does all this tell you about making ideas happen?

It's the same answer to all three questions: the ability to infect others with your own enthusiasm. Bill himself has said that sharing his enthusiasm is what he does best and he's not alone in this fundamental belief.

'I consider my ability to arouse enthusiasm among men the greatest asset I possess.'

Charles Schwabb, US industrialist

———————

'Flaming enthusiasm, backed up by horse sense and persistence, is the quality that most frequently makes for success.'

Dale Carnegie, developer of famous courses on self-improvement, salesmanship, corporate training, public speaking and interpersonal skills

———————

'People will only want to supply you, finance you and buy from you if you have confidence, faith and passion in your product and idea.'

Karen Bilimoria, founder and chief executive of Cobra Beer (from Sodowick and Watts, 2005)

———————

'Enthusiasm is an unstoppable force and one of the essential ingredients of starting a business successfully.'

Dame Anita Roddick (from Sodowick and Watts, 2005)

———————

Imagine what it must have been like to be around Bill Gates when he first created Microsoft. He started out with just an idea: to put a PC in every home and on every desk. It must have seemed impossible to everybody at the time, but Bill's enthusiasm would have been infectious. His idea became Microsoft's corporate mission for its first 25 years. It was an idea that was worth tens of billions of dollars to him personally but countless more to the global economy.

The ability to express your enthusiasm and instil it in others is the key to turning your big idea into a reality. The word *enthusiasm* derives from the Greek word *entheos*, which translates as 'the quality displayed by those possessed by a god'. You don't have to believe in one deity, let alone multiple gods to understand what the Greeks meant. A man or a woman possessed by enthusiasm is a truly unstoppable force.

Imagine how Tim Berners-Lee feels now as he sees the World Wide Web sweep all before it in transforming the lives of billions of people. In 1989, the Web existed as merely an idea. It was only given life because of Tim's enthusiasm for it.

> *'The dream behind the Web is of a common information space in which we communicate by sharing information. Its universality is essential: the fact that a hypertext link can point to anything, be it personal, local or global, be it draft or highly polished. There was a second part of the dream, too, dependent on the Web being so generally used that it became a realistic mirror (or in fact the primary embodiment) of the ways in which we work and play and socialize. That was that once the state of our interactions was online – we could then use computers to help us analyse it, make sense of what we are doing, where we individually fit in, and how we can better work together.'*

Tim Berners-Lee

Tim's powerful use of the word dream is a very common way in which entrepreneurs express their ambitions.

Do something

Write down a few sentences about your own dream, whatever it is. It doesn't matter how you express it – nobody else will ever see what you write. Your dream might simply be the act of giving birth to a new idea or it might be the thought of creating your own company.

A good way to think about this is to consider how a journalist might write about your success story in ten years' time. What did you achieve and how? What was the secret of your success?

I often get participants to do this exercise in my workshops. It's a great way for people to be clear about what they want and what really matters to them. Achieving that clarity is extremely important as a source of focus when you are moving forward. It also gives them a taste of what success feels like – there's no greater motivator than that!

First steps

People don't get enthused by your idea, people get enthused by *you* – but only when they are convinced that you are prepared to live your dream. You must therefore prove to them that you are going to take the first step to make it happen, however tentative.

In 1988, I had taken the first step towards making a dream of my own into a reality. I was working as part of a team on a project for Midland Bank (now HSBC). We were creating something new and innovative: a new bank with a new brand. We called it Raincloud at that time but it was ultimately to be Firstdirect – the world's first telephone bank, which would provide outstanding levels of service to its customers, 24 hours a day, seven days a week. By negating branches, recruiting and training only the best staff, and ensuring it was simply the most exciting place to work, we were determined to change the way people banked forever.

While it was easy for me to be enthusiastic about making this happen, it was also easy to be daunted by the prospect of turning it into a profitable business. I was immersed in deep thought about all this one Saturday while walking around the Cotswold town of Chipping Camden with my wife, Sue. She wasn't entirely happy because I was, admittedly, less than exuberant company that day. I followed her into one of the antique shops and began sifting through some old maps when she thrust a wooden frame into my hands. It contained a piece of paper that read:

'Whatever you can do or dream you can, begin it. Boldness has genius, power and magic in it. Begin it now.'

Johann Wolfgang von Goethe

'There you are – there's your answer' she said. 'Stop making a fuss and get on with it.'

That frame has since occupied pride of place on the wall in my office. The words had instantly moved me, although I had no idea who Goethe was at the time. I know now that he was a 19th century German poet and philosopher, and much more besides. His advice to the would-be entrepreneur is excellent.

One small step

Initially, all it takes to get started is enthusiasm, bold commitment and determination. So if you have an idea, why not make the conscious decision to stop dreaming and start it now? If you prefer, the more prosaic 'Stop making a fuss and just get on with it' is also pretty good advice.

The following Monday I decided to do just that. I decided to start the dream that was to become the world's most famous telephone bank, an iconic consumer brand that to this day still stands for the best service you can get from a bank. I called the team together and said, 'Right, we *are* going to make this happen. I have no idea how, but we are going to go for it.' The next thing I knew, we not only had approval from Midland Bank, but we also had the funds and the show had begun.

Immediately I found myself immersed in chaos – improvising, hustling and loving every minute of it. I found myself thinking alternately 'This is great, we're really on our way' followed by 'Oh my God, I can't do this – how did I ever get into it?'

Back then I relied on instinct and intuition to get things done. But a lifetime spent creating businesses has taught me to do things a bit differently. I now know it takes a lot of courage to take the first step in getting an idea into the world. Everyone is nervous and frightened. I certainly was – panic-stricken might actually be a better description. But what I know now is that while there may be no guarantee of success, you can stack the odds heavily in your favour by learning from others.

I also know that ultimately, win or lose, you will be left with a wealth of memories and fantastic experiences. You will never regret living your dream if you live it full on, holding nothing back. If you don't take some risks you never get anywhere. The rewards can be immense – and I don't just mean financially.

Reap the rewards

In my experience, there is no greater feeling in business than seeing an idea come kicking into the world. I remember feeling this way just before the launch of Firstdirect when I gave my family a tour of the call centre. There was a fantastic buzz about the place – hundreds of highly trained and motivated people bustling around, computers everywhere, systems whirring impressively. Walking around, I felt both immensely proud and totally astonished that we had managed to pull it all together. Just an idea and a bunch of ordinary people had created all of this. It made me feel as though we had really done something extraordinary. It made me feel extraordinary. My kids were even more astonished that their dad, an ordinary sort of a bloke, had been the cause of all of this.

> *'A really innovative and exceptional team turned the vision into reality. I still remember the launch party – hundreds of people celebrating months of great cooperation, determined persever-ance and clever creativity. I looked back that night on the experi-ence as a real gift in my life and wished that everyone could have that one opportunity, as we did, of trying to build something thoughtful, intelligent and different – and to be able to share it with thousands of people. We were all very exhilarated ...'*

Steve Mayers, who came up with the original idea that led to Firstdirect and was the Senior Marketing Manager on the launch team

---

Everyone can be extraordinary

Ordinary people who are prepared to do extraordinary things – that's what it takes to get big ideas into the world. You don't need superhuman intelligence or superpowers of any description.

Yes, there are a few superhumans around: Gates and Berners-Lee definitely fall into that category. But your normal entrepre-neur is just that – normal:

- Seb Pole, who created the exciting Pukka Herbs.
- Terry Rhodes, who was the strategic brains behind the mobile phone company Celtel.

- Alistair Lukies, who created the mobile banking success story MoniLink.
- Stef Calcraft, who created the stunningly innovative advertising agency Mother.
- David Kelley, who created the celebrated design and innovation consultancy, Ideo.
- Barbara Cassani, who created the low-cost airline Go.
- Richard Reed, who created Innocent Drinks.

If you met any of them at party, you wouldn't find them vastly different from yourself. What makes them extraordinary is two things, both of which are easily available to you. Firstly, they had genuine enthusiasm for their dream, which they used to infect others. Secondly, they were bold enough to begin their dream.

Pukka power

I have come across countless examples of ordinary people being extraordinary by choice.

But Sebastian Pole is one of my favourites. He is a young herbalist who had studied the use of Indian herbal remedies and wanted to use them in his UK practice. The problem was that many of the classic Ayurvedic formulae were not reliably available in the UK and many of the Indian herbs were grown by subsistence farmers who relied on pesticides to get a decent crop. The pesticides hardly met the Ayurvedic ideal of natural purity.

Sebastian's problem was shared by many naturopaths and complementary practitioners in the UK, but Sebastian alone had the courage to do something about it. He developed a network of organic suppliers in India and Sri Lanka, imported the herbs, and manufactured traditional Ayurvedic remedies for distribution in Europe. His company Pukka Herbs is the living embodiment of his dream.

> 'Pukka Herbs is dedicated to promoting an integrated relationship between people and our natural world where the value of what we do is based on sustainability, where the environmental and social impact is considered along with "the price", and where the authenticity of the tradition that we represent is respected throughout all that we do. Ayurveda strives to create the best health for the individual, the community and the environment. At Pukka Herbs we are doing all that we can to make this dream a reality for all of us.'
>
> Sebastian Pole

It's too early to say how much money Seb will make from Pukka, but he's truly living his dream.

Another notable example is Terry Rhodes. I first met him when he was a young economist in the strategy department at Mercury Communications. One day our attentions turned to the future of telephony.

'What about the Africans?' Terry posed. 'They're going to need phones – mobile phones, probably.'

I thought his idea was interesting, but after debating the merits I soon forgot about the entire conversation. Terry, on the other hand, teamed up with entrepreneur Mo Ibrahim to create Celtel, which built a series of mobile telephone companies across Africa. When Celtel was sold in 2005 for a little over $3bn, Terry was well rewarded for living his dream.

Big ideas

A lot of people tell me about their big idea, followed by all the reasons they can't make it happen. Humans seem to be uniquely inventive when it comes to finding excuses about why it's not possible to do something. But by far the most common and de-structive excuse is 'My idea is so simple – I'm not sure it's worth that much.'

Let me assure you that simple ideas are sometimes the most powerful – they don't even have to be original. It's how you im-plement them that counts.

> *'If you never have a single great idea in your life but become skilled at executing the great ideas of others, you can succeed beyond your wildest dreams. Seek them out and make them work. They do not have to be your ideas. Execution is all in this regard.'*

Felix Dennis, entrepreneur and author of *How to Get Rich*

Banking by telephone wasn't a particularly complex idea; it wasn't even that original. When Firstdirect was conceived, a few US banks had already set up telephone banking centres to provide an additional service channel that supplemented their branch networks. The genius of Firstdirect was that we created a whole new bank out of the idea of telephone banking, removing the need for branches altogether. It was also fantastically well implemented.

Think of eBay – it's basically the interactive version of small ads in local newspapers. There were Internet search engines be-fore Google, but Google's implementation was vastly superior. Post-it notes were a simple idea – just bits of paper with glue on the back. Digital music and MP3 players existed before Apple created iTunes and the iPod – Apple transformed an existing simple idea into a multibillion business with great design and great implementation.

So don't despair if you think your idea isn't exactly rocket sci-ence. Simple ideas are often the best; success lies in implement-ing them better than anyone else has before.

Do something

There are no excuses left for you now. You don't need to be su-perhuman – you only need a simple idea and it doesn't even have to be original. So go ahead, start to unleash the power you were born with – the power to introduce a new idea into the world.

It only takes two things, both of which can be achieved in a single first step. You need to be bold enough to begin your dream and you need to learn how to infect others with your enthusiasm for it.

So begin by telling a few people what you intend to do. Speak with commitment and passion, with no apologies or excuses. It's extraordinary how powerful such a statement can be. Keep making your statement of intention until you notice your self-belief and enthusiasm growing and beginning to infect others.

Here's how.

Create a statement, something like one of the following:

- 'I have a new business idea – I'm going to find a way to make it happen and I'm going to make money out of it. Within three months, I'll have the show on the road.' Produce a one-minute pitch on the idea itself.
- 'I've been working on this new idea/business and it's a bit stuck at the moment, but no one should doubt for a minute that I'm going to make it happen. Within three months, everything will be flying.' Produce a one-minute elevator pitch on the idea and a one-minute pitch on the current problems.
- 'I'm going to start a new business that will make me millions. I'm not sure what yet, but I'll have kicked it off in three months' time.' Produce a one-minute pitch on how excited you are at the prospect of finally doing something you always wanted to do.

First of all, practise your statements and pitches in front of a mirror. When you feel ready, move on to your friends and colleagues. I don't recommend your boss, partners or family members at this stage – it's too early for that sort of challenge.

After you've made your pitch, consider just how enthusiastic and genuine you felt and how your audience responded. Mark yourself on a scale of one to ten. It may take several pitches to several people but when you get up to eight out of ten, you're on your way. You have unleashed something really spectacular, the power of a man or woman possessed by enthusiasm – what the ancient Greeks called *the power of the gods*.

You have accessed your raw power. It should help reinforce the lessons of this chapter and make them real for you. If you do choose to start a business of your own, you will find yourself having to express your enthusiasm to many people over and over again. The more skilled and practised you are at infecting others with your enthusiasm, the more successful you are likely to be.

2

Star in your own soap opera

'All the world's a stage,
And all the men and women merely players:
They have their exits and their entrances;
And one man in his time plays many parts.'

William Shakespeare, *As You Like It* (Act II Scene 7)

A matter of mindset

There's no doubt that Shakespeare was right. Not only in the existential sense, but he's spot on when it comes to the business world too. Like it or not, if you have been bold enough to take the first step towards making your dream a reality, then you have become the leading actor in a drama.

You might well be wondering what makes it a drama. What role does the leading actor have to play and what exactly does all this have to do with making big ideas happen?

One humid Friday evening in July 2000, the answer to all those questions was as clear to me as the sparkling Manhattan skyline. I was in a helicopter with two colleagues and a couple of investment bankers, sweeping between skyscrapers in an exhilarating ride of celebration. I was ready to take a bow at the conclusion of a drama that I had initiated almost exactly three years beforehand. Egg had just completed its initial public offering. We had sold the last few shares that afternoon in New York and we would list on the London Stock Exchange the following week at a value of £1.3bn.

It really all started in April 1997. I was working with Tracy Goss, the world's leading expert on transformational leadership and executive reinvention. She asked me a great question: 'What would you love to do next in business if anything was possible?'

I thought for a while before I told her that I would persuade the Prudential Corporation (for whom I was working at the time) to invest in a revolutionary new financial services company that would be intensely customer-focused and would utilize emerging technology such as the Internet and digital TV. This company would appeal to at least ten million customers in the UK. I wanted to build the business, float it on the stock exchange at a value of more than £1bn and retire as Chief Executive before the end of the year 2000.

Then I laughed, because everything about that idea seemed implausible. Not only was Prudential one of Britain's most conservative companies, but the notion of attracting ten million customers to a revolutionary, digital age concept when only 500,000 people were connected to the Internet in the UK was ludicrous.

But as I sat in that helicopter three years after laughing at myself for writing down a bunch of nonsense, I realized that literally everything I had desired but declared impossible had actually happened. Prudential had invested in a new bank that we called Egg. It had been lauded by the *Financial Times* as 'fundamentally changing the landscape of UK financial services'. It was now the

world's biggest Internet bank, with more than a million customers, and was growing rapidly. Our market research showed that
the proposition appealed to at least ten million people in the UK.
We had just floated the company on the Stock Exchange and it
was worth £1.3bn. I was retiring as CEO at the end of the year to
take on a part-time role as Vice-Chairman.

My thoughts three years before actually formed the final
chapter of a story that I had crafted before it had even begun.
That final chapter provided inspiration to me and countless others throughout the dramatic twists and turns that finally led to
our successful outcome. And believe me, it was a drama. There
was knife-edge tension at times as we tottered precariously on
the terribly thin line that divides success and failure. Much of
it happened in the public eye and was faithfully reported week
after week in the national media. Putting a big idea into the world
is not for those who want a quiet and predictable life.

Dull or dramatic?

No big idea gets into the world smoothly. Logically speaking, if
an idea is really easy to implement, then it's probably not going
to make a lot of money. Big ideas fundamentally change the
world and change is always fraught with obstacles and always
attracts enemies.

The truth is, all of my business adventures have felt like dramas to me. I tend to think of them as more like soap operas than
grand operas, but they have been dramas nonetheless. Every one
has been full of the trials and tribulations of everyday life, pep-
pered with apparently immovable obstacles and enemy actions
that interfered with what I had planned, and challenged my very
sanity. They have also been full of the magic of human life: humour, courage, despair, anger, pride, friendship, great triumphs,
epic celebrations, fun and extraordinary good fortune.

Experience has led me to love this drama, to embrace it and
turn it to my advantage. The joy of being an entrepreneur is that

at least it's you that writes the script. You are the star of your own soap opera – not an extra in someone else's. The sense of control this gives you over your own destiny is an important psychological weapon.

David Magliano, Director of Marketing for London 2012 (the organization that successfully bid to host the 2012 Olympic Games) found exactly this. He masterminded the crucial presentation in Singapore before the final decision. This race has been described as the fiercest competitive pitch of all time.

'When it came to winning the 2012 bid to host the Olympic Games, we wrote our own script in every sense of the word. With just 45 minutes to convince the International Olympic Committee that London was the right choice from five world-class cities, we needed to break the mould of everything that had gone before. Our research was obsessive. We studied 12 years' worth of footage of previous presentations from the Olympic archives. It was a laborious process but proved instrumental to our success. We noticed that every previous bid had taken the same approach – it made the city, its people and its technical plans the 'hero' of the presentation. We thought our opponents would beat us hands down if we did the same. So we decided that London was going to address a real problem facing the Olympic Movement – the challenge of reaching young people and connecting them with the inspirational power of the Games. Everyone expected us to showcase red London buses and Buckingham Palace. We surprised them. Instead we focused on children as the legacy of sport. At the time it was a risky strategy, which met with huge resistance from some people, but evidently it paid off.'

David Magliano

David is a true disciple of the power of writing your own script in order to achieve success. The mindset of being both the star and the script writer of your own soap opera is very powerful in making your dream a reality.

By writing the final chapter first, as I did about Egg in 1997, you can set yourself an apparently impossible challenge without needing to worry too early on about how you are going to get there. You create a destination, a guiding star that gives you a unique kind of certainty – the certainty that comes from knowing that whatever challenges and circumstances you meet, however far you get blown off course, you will always know which direction to take next.

So what part are you going to write for yourself? What about the role of exactly the sort of leader that makes your dream come true and puts millions in the bank – do you think that might help?

Apparently impossible challenges

I first discovered the power of aiming for apparently impossible goals when I was at Firstdirect in 1988. I still remember the regular waves of panic that flowed over me after I got the go-ahead to build it. Thankfully, though, panic alternated with the exhilaration of being in control of my own destiny. I was going to make something happen, something new and exciting, something that would not have happened without me.

The original team of five that created the idea had been supplemented by a secretary, an administrative assistant, a consultant and two bankers. There were just the ten of us in some tatty old offices near the Tower of London. None of us had ever created or run a business before. As we struggled to focus on what we needed to do and realized the real scale of the task, it occurred to me that this would make a great soap opera – a long-running serial concerned with everyday life but with recurring conflicts and crises where the characters come and go.

So I started to keep a diary. I started to speculate on who would play the major parts if it were ever filmed, who would be the cast, who would be the crew and how the storyline would unfurl. As we relaxed over a few drinks one evening, my private musings evolved into a game the whole team played. We would each write down who we would like to play us in a film and also our choice of actor for each other. It was the differences in view that made this game fun. Someone chose Harrison Ford to play themselves, while the rest of the team had chosen Danny de Vito.

It might sound like a strange game, but it really helped us to take a step back and stay objective about what we were creating. It also helped us realize that we were in control; there was no one to tell us what to do or how to do it. This was especially true when hurdles more insurmountable than we'd ever imagined suddenly emerged.

This first happened in October 1988, when we sat down to write a list of tasks which needed tackling immediately. Judging by the increasingly burdened expressions as I looked around the room, it was far longer than any of us had ever expected. We needed:

- to recruit and train a few hundred people to do something that had never been done before – handle every banking request you could think of by telephone
- somewhere to put them – 120,000 square feet on a single floor – so we could have everybody working together
- computer and telephone systems.
- an IT Director and team, a Marketing Director and team, an HR Director and team, and a Finance Director and team
- to define our products and build them
- a name, a brand and some designs
- processes, printing and dispatch, credit cards, and debit cards
- advertising agencies and ad campaigns
- a Management Information System.

The longer we thought about it, the longer the list became. We had agreed with our investor that we would launch exactly one year later. Considering our task list, October 1989 seemed as though it was just a blink away. So, intent on not going back and renegotiating, we tried to formulate a plan to meet our deadline. The overriding feeling among the team at the time was that it wouldn't and couldn't work – we'd never fit all those tasks into the time we had available.

I had a shocking revelation at the time that has stayed with me ever since. If I appeared enthusiastic and confident about our eventual success, however gloomy the current situation looked, then the team were happy and things moved forward. The converse was also true; if I was unhappy and despondent, things stood still or even regressed. I soon learnt that enthusiasm for an idea needs to be recreated every day, for yourself and for the whole team; however you are feeling.

How you do this is up to you, whether it's a matter of creating a bold exciting environment through team bonding or incentives.

'In 1996, Selfridges underwent an exciting transformation managed by Vittorio Raddice. We had the joint goal of creating something exciting and dynamic. Vittorio was fantastic at galvanizing people and getting them excited about bold new things. By unquestioningly challenging the norms of current retail standards, employing cutting edge talent and alternative approaches to anything from architecture to advertising, you couldn't help but be enthused by our mission. We also gave people the opportunity to demonstrate and prove their enthusiasm by abolishing uniforms. It soon became apparent who was committed to our mission and intent on representing the store in the best possible light.'

Nick Cross, ex-Marketing Director at Selfridges during its business transformation under Vittorio Raddice

---

'Our environment is a key tool in exciting and motivating people at Mother. The office is organized around a 300-foot round desk, like a racing track. The space is bright with lots of colour, no walls and no cliques, because people move around every few weeks. We give people free reign to express themselves and equally to attract the kind of creative people who would thrive in this open-plan environment. We look after our people making it feel like a home from home – beyond highly competitive salary packages, everybody gets a free lunch and an extra day off each year they stay, as well as having photos of their mums on the walls and their business cards. We pride ourselves on our sense of fun, humour and creativity, and each Janaury the Mother London, Buenos Aires and New York agencies all meet to ski together. If you want to escape of course you can work from anywhere, but it is no suprise that most people love the office, and this is one of our biggest secrets of success.'

Stef Calcraft, founder of the highly innovative advertising agency Mother

---

'I like to think I challenge Dyson people – to come up with new ideas and do things differently. Equally, I like them to challenge me. Although we all have job titles no one is restricted by hierarchy or formalities when it comes to fresh thinking.'

James Dyson, inventor of the dual cyclone bagless vacuum cleaner

---

The problem

But the problem for me at that early time at Firstdirect was how to spread confidence in our eventual success when it looked like an impossible challenge to me as well. The answer came into my head from an unlikely source. Back in the 1960s, an exuberant football manager named Tommy Docherty built a young and exciting Chelsea team. After a triumphant season it looked certain that they would be promoted to the top division. But in the last few weeks, it all fell apart for them: they lost form and, with four matches to go, it looked like they had blown their chances. Docherty's answer was to take them all out for a celebration, telling them to pretend they had already achieved success. It worked. After their night out, Chelsea recovered and were eventually promoted.

Inspired by Docherty, I decided to celebrate Firstdirect's success before it had actually happened. To make this real for my colleagues, I also wrote the last chapter of the Firstdirect soap opera. I called it the *brand book* – a description of the company and brand we were setting out to create.

I wrote that in three years' time, Firstdirect would be universally acknowledged as the finest bank in the world. I described how it would feel when we got there, what the role of each department would be and I stated confidently that all this was made possible by a successful launch in October 1989 as planned. I circulated the brand book, and took everyone out to celebrate.

'Let's have the party before we start,' I told them. 'That way, if we fail at least we get to have some fun.'

In doing all of this I created a destination that everyone could aim for – it was an impossible challenge but also an inspirational one that made everyone determined to hit the first milestone of our October launch. I had also achieved a change in my mindset and that of the team. We went from 'It's not possible, we can't do it' to 'It's really desirable, we can do it, get out of our way'. And of course we did hit that first impossible goal of an on-budget launch, right on time.

> *'I couldn't believe it all came together so successfully. There was so much to do. When Mike first recruited me for the job I thought he was joking when he told me the timescale. When he said he was serious, I remember feeling shocked then elated – I could be part of a team which took on something extraordinary. We not only took it on, we made it happen.'*

Peter Murley, HR Director on the Firstdirect launch team

Audacious goals

This power of committing yourself to a goal without having a clue how to get there was given academic respectability by Stanford University professors James Collins and Jerry Porras in their book *Built to Last*. After painstakingly researching the distinguishing characteristics of enduringly great companies, they concluded that the majority have a long history of committing themselves to what they called big hairy audacious goals (BHAGs, pronounced 'bee-hags').

> *'A BHAG is clear and compelling and serves as a unifying focal point of effort, often creating immense team spirit. It energizes people. It reaches out and grabs them in the gut. It is tangible, energizing and highly focused.'*

James Collins and Jerry Porras, authors of *Built to Last*

Among their many examples, the BHAG that stood out for me was IBM in the 1960s: to commit to a $5bn gamble in order to meet the emerging needs of their customers. That gamble created the first modern computer and laid the foundation for IBM's 20-year dominance of the computer industry.

A Bold and Inspiring Future

Although I like the concept of a BHAG, it's not a term I often use. Instead I talk to executives about the need to invent and articulate a Bold and Inspiring Future. What follows is the best articulation of a Bold and Inspiring Future I have ever come across. When I'm rubbing my head because I have to plough through endless budget reviews, I always try to keep this inspirational and persuasive speech in mind.

> 'We choose to go to the moon. We choose to go to the moon in this decade and do the other things, not because they are easy, but because they are hard, because that goal will serve to organize and measure the best of our energies and skills, because that challenge is one that we are willing to accept, one we are unwilling to postpone, and one which we intend to win, and the others, too.

> 'But if I were to say, my fellow citizens, that we shall send to the moon, 240,000 miles away from the control station in Houston, a giant rocket more than 300 feet tall, the length of this football field, made of new metal alloys, some of which have not yet been invented, capable of standing heat and stresses several times more than have ever been experienced, fitted together with a precision better than the finest watch, carrying all the equipment needed for propulsion, guidance, control, communications, food and survival, on an untried mission, to an unknown

celestial body, and then return it safely to earth, re-entering the atmosphere at speeds of over 25,000 miles per hour, causing heat about half that of the temperature of the sun – almost as hot as it is here today – and do all this, and do it right, and do it first before this decade is out – then we must be bold.

'I'm the one who is doing all the work, so we just want you to stay cool for a minute.'

John F. Kennedy, 12 September 1962 (cited by John T. Woolley and Gerhard Peters, The American Presidency Project [online])

Do something

Think of a leader who has inspired you. What was it that really turned you on about them? Can you remember a particular speech or communication that really stands out for you?

Now think of an achievement of your own that you are most proud of: something you took on that seemed really hard – perhaps impossible – to you at the time, but where you battled on and succeeded.

It's worth getting both these things firmly in your mind because they can continue to provide sources of inspiration in the inevitable dull and dark moments you will face as you start to put your ideas into action.

Motivate yourself and others

Within reason, the bolder and more inspiring the future to which you have committed yourself, the more people seem to step up to the plate and display fantastic effort and creativity in getting results. Remember, though, people must really believe they have a chance of success – however irrational this belief may seem to others.

The first question I am always asked at public seminars is 'But how do I know if I've set a challenge that's so completely impossible no one will ever believe in it?'

The answer that almost every entrepreneur will give you is 'instinct' – you'll know somewhere deep inside whether it has a chance of working or not.

> *'How can you know when things are going to fail? You cannot. Nobody has 20:20 future vision. But if you are running the business, you will certainly know much earlier than anyone else, providing you are willing to stare reality in the face – which many executives and entrepreneurs are not.'*

Felix Dennis, 2006

Another tip is to watch people carefully as you describe your impossible challenge. If you are getting a lot of energy and reaction (positive or negative), you are probably in the right territory. A lack of energy or easy agreement means you have either gone too far or you are not stretching your idea enough. You can also use an approach that I got from Tracy Goss, the world's foremost expert on transformational leadership. She told me to write down the five major challenges I thought I would have to overcome to achieve my goals. If wrestling with those challenges is your idea of a good time, then you are on the right track.

Mercury Communications and the Imagine programme

The boldest and most inspiring future I have ever set out to create was at Mercury Communications. I was headhunted to take over as CEO in 1991. Mercury was a subsidiary of Cable & Wireless and had been created in 1981 to provide competition to BT.

At the time I joined, Mercury was being described as one of the fastest-growing large companies in Europe. It had just reached a milestone of £1bn in revenues, but it was under increasing margin and competitive pressure from BT and other new entrants to the market. At the same time the telecommunications market was changing fundamentally, in line with the dawning of the new digital age.

My first move at Mercury was to commit to building a famous consumer brand and a large consumer telephony business. Until then, Mercury had been largely focused on the business market. The consumer business was very successful and went on to net Cable & Wireless £2.5bn when it was sold in 1997.

For Mercury as a whole, though, I came up with 'Imagine' – a complete strategy for the new digital world. With the help of some organizational change consultants, the management team got together and produced a vision for a Bold and Inspiring Future for Mercury set three years in the future. Here's what we came up with:

> *'By 2007, everybody agrees that Mercury has inspired communication beyond your imagination, bringing people, information and entertainment into the palm of your hand.'*

You will recognize this technique by now – writing the final chapter first. I employed consultants to help because I was trying to transform a large existing company rather than creating a new one, and that was virgin territory for me.

The Imagine programme attempted to engage the whole company in a programme of organizational reinvention, innovation and entrepreneurship. The general view was that it was bold and audacious. McKinsey was quoted as saying that it was the most audacious change programme they had ever seen.

'Everybody still talks about Imagine all these years later – for all of us it was the most dynamic environment we have ever experienced at work.'

Ben Timmons, November 2007, Strategy Manager at Mercury in the early 1990s, now Director of Business Development at Qualcomm Europe

---

However, as with any bold innovation, it also had its share critics and inspired a certain amount of controversy.

'Since September last year, 9000 of Mercury's 11,000 staff have visited three huge canvas igloos erected in a car park at the National Exhibition Centre in Birmingham. At night the igloos are bathed in light and are visible to motorists on the M42; by day they house 100 Mercury staff for up to ten hours during intense training programmes, known as "ignition" sessions.

'The sessions, designed to unleash "awesome velocity" motivation in employees, involve much applause, emotional debate and candid disclosures, accompanied by all the sound effects and stage props that are standard fare to many American-style cults.

'Not surprisingly, some employees have emerged from the igloos, or domes as they are properly called, claiming to have been brainwashed.'

The Sunday Times, 24 April 1994

Regardless of the scepticism and the eventual fallout, Mercury used Imagine to dream up and prototype many of the products and services we now take for granted in the digital age. This included Internet browsers, search tools, interactive TV, local and wide area wireless networks, and a device we called the Smart Palm. This was an online handheld gadget that put people, information and entertainment directly in the palm of your hand. Nokia has now launched almost exactly what we had in mind with its N95 smartphone, some 14 years after our first prototype.

Evidently we were somewhat ahead of our time. I am under no doubt that if we had been able to keep going during Imagine, we could have had spectacular success during the next ten years. We just needed to step back and approach the ideas behind our prototypes a step at a time. If we had done that, it's not hard to imagine Mercury becoming a global force as the Internet exploded in the late 1990s.

However, I was concerned about the controversy surrounding Imagine, by the lack of near-term opportunities to generate revenues from our ideas and by the struggle to achieve profit targets given the highly competitive marketplace. I began to reduce the amount of time and money we were putting into it in favour of some profitable short-term initiatives. It looked to everyone as though I had given up on it.

It's hard for a CEO to survive a change of direction like that and, in November 2004, I was asked to step aside into another role at Cable & Wireless. I was asked to take charge of a small innovation and venture unit based in Silicon Valley. I didn't do that for very long, though – it was just four short months before the desire to create another company took over and I left to join Prudential and eventually create Egg.

I never regretted what I had attempted to do at Mercury. With the benefit of hindsight I would never have given up on Imagine. If I knew what I know now, I would have amended my approach, gritted my teeth and seen it through. Had I stayed committed and enthusiastic, I believe the board would have backed me.

That's a big lesson I want to give you: Once you have got people enrolled in a Bold and Inspiring Future, you must not give up on it. Change your approach by all means, but stay committed to getting to that last chapter. If you are destined to fail, it's better to fail because others stopped you – not because you stopped yourself.

> ## Business coaching
>
> I was introduced to the concept of business coaching during the Imagine programme by one of the advisors we were employing. His name is Gordon Starr and he is a San Francisco-based expert in transforming organizational culture. At its most basic, a business coach seeks to provide insights that enable executives to achieve their goals more quickly and with less effort than would otherwise be the case. This is done for the most part through conversation. At its most powerful, as employed by Gordon Starr or Tracy Goss for example, coaching provides a deep existential insight to what drives us and how we make choices. Discovering this is very empowering for most people and it allows them to step beyond previous limitations to new levels of accomplishment.

Being the leader you need to be

So turn your thoughts to what role you are going to write for yourself into your personal soap opera. As the creator of the soap opera that was the overall Imagine programme, I had to consider my own role as leader. I based my role on what I already knew about many successful entrepreneurs:

- They are strong leaders, comfortable with taking control of situations and making key decisions.
- They build and surround themselves with great teams.

- They are not afraid to appear unreasonable in order to get what they need.
- They are bold improvisers, not cautious strategists.
- They are comfortable with using their intuition rather than needing to be analytical about everything.

If this already sounds like you, then that's fantastic – give yourself permission to stay this way even if others tell you to change. Remember that you are the star in your own soap opera. You write the script so you can be whoever you want to be.

However, if you are not naturally unreasonable, then you will need to get comfortable with the fact that at times you will have to act this way in order to get what you need. You are going to have to keep a tight control on the key decisions in order to stay on track. And if you are uncomfortable basing some decisions on intuition, start to trust yourself right now.

Do something

Write a few lines from the first paragraph of the final chapter of your very own soap opera. Do it right now and you will have taken a big step towards getting those millions in the bank.

Write down what will be true about your idea in three or five years' time that is not true today.

Write down what's important to you about the way you go about making that happen.

If you haven't found your idea yet, you can come back to this exercise after Chapter 4 ('Making million-pound ideas'), or just pick a product or service that you use in your personal or business life and imagine how you would reinvent it so that it's perfect for you.

If you are working with others, get them involved – but it's your accountability so you have the final say.

Here's an example:

> The final chapter of the story of my current company Garlik contains the following statement:
> *'Everybody agrees that they have a digital identity that it is important and it needs to be managed and protected.*
> *'We made this happen by illuminating the digital world so that individuals and their families have more insight and more power over the way their personal information is used.'*
> That is not true about digital identity today – our soap opera is the unfolding story of how Garlik is making it happen.

Writing the final chapter for real

When you get started on actually making your idea happen, you should put serious effort into writing the last chapter in full. It need not be long; maybe only a page.

Remember:

- The final chapter is about what you have accomplished in three to five years' time and how you went about it.
- You don't need detailed financial goals right now.
- Your accomplishments should fall well outside what you know how to achieve.
- What you write should be clear, self-explanatory, bold and exciting to you and your collaborators – it doesn't necessarily need to mean anything to the outside world.

When you are really ready to start your business, write that last chapter first and inspire yourself into turning your dream into a reality.

3

Critics who count

'It's not the critic who counts, not the man who points out how the strong man stumbled, or where the doer of deeds could have done better. The credit belongs to the man who is actually in the arena; whose face is marred by dust and sweat and blood; who strives valiantly; who errs and comes short again and again; who knows great enthusiasms, great devotions and spends himself in a worthy cause; who at the best, knows in the end the triumph of high achievement; and who at the worst if he fails, at least fails while daring greatly, so that his place shall never be with those cold and timid souls who know neither victory nor defeat.'

Theodore Roosevelt

The first time I read these words was in October 1994. It was towards the end of my time at Mercury. Imagine was grinding to a halt because the stream of new products we were hoping for was well behind schedule. Sale of our existing products were struggling as BT turned up the competitive pressure and meeting that year's profit target looked like a bit of a challenge, to say the least. I was dealing with a storm of internal and external criticism. One of the consultants advising Mercury at that time emailed me the Roosevelt quote, adding: 'Don't let the buggers get you down'.

Absolutely right, I thought. What have critics ever achieved anyway?

But I couldn't have been more wrong. I later discovered that my attitude at the time was entirely erroneous; critics do count, and if you have followed my advice so far, you will soon find out why for yourself.

By now you should have stopped dreaming and actually taken the first step towards living your dream. You will have learned how to express enthusiasm for your idea and infect others with it. You will have written the first few lines of the final chapter of your soap opera and you will be about to take the first steps toward achieving your Bold and Inspiring Future.

At some point you will have to start talking seriously to others about your plans. You will need to get people to work with you. You may well have business partners and suppliers to talk to and you may need to raise money. Everyone will be asking, 'What's your plan and what does your product look like?'

Whatever plan and initial design you come up with, no matter how rudimentary or how complex, one thing is guaranteed – you will find critics swarming all over them. When people have to make serious decisions about whether to come on board, they will temper their enthusiasm with rational assessments. A fundamental part of this process involves criticism. Statements such as 'That will never work' will proliferate and soon you will know every little thing that's apparently wrong with your idea. It's a natural reaction – we all do it, myself included.

That'll never work!

I was spending the winter of 1987 in Helsinki doing some consultancy for a Finnish bank. My work led me to visit a small company called Nokia. Hardly known outside Finland, Nokia was a timber company that had recently moved into consumer electronics with a range of TVs and banking terminals – hence my visit.

What really captured my interest was the mobile telephone that they had just begun to manufacture. Although this was the first phone you could actually carry around with you, it was the size and weight of a brick, and you needed a small suitcase to carry it around. I almost laughed out loud when a Nokia executive explained that their vision was a world where everyone had a phone in their pocket that could be used anywhere.

That's never going to work, I thought to myself. Who would carry that thing around? Reception will be awful and it will drive everyone mad. Who the hell needs a phone in their pocket anyway? And even if there was a real need, how could this little Finnish company ever beat the telecom giants?

Twenty years later and a pocket without a mobile phone is a distinct rarity. It's a truly ubiquitous product, transforming modern life beyond belief. Nokia clearly made their vision happen. In the process, they transformed themselves into one of the world's leading technology companies, overtaking a multitude of much stronger telecommunications suppliers. Nokia's rise to global leadership is one of the most impressive business stories of the last 50 years.

The best-kept secret in business

No person or idea is immune from criticism. I have noticed myself that talking about what's wrong and who is to blame is one of the dominant conversations in the world. But while we don't mind criticizing others, or even ourselves at times, we hate it when criticism is directed at us. 'What do they know?' we think. 'They should try doing this job.' We reject what they have to say without much further thought.

Most of the time, this reaction is exactly right. Although criticisms may irritate you, they won't make a difference to the results you get. However, there is an exception to that rule: a situation where a proactive strategy is going to make a fundamental difference to your chance of success. This exception is the best-kept secret in business. It is particularly relevant when you're bringing a new idea into the world. It happens when someone looks at your idea thoughtfully and says 'That will never work'.

With any luck, your critic will go on to tell you all the reasons why it won't work. Instead of being discouraged or ignoring them, you should prick up your ears, get out your pen and frantically take notes. 'That will never work' is the experts' verdict on the majority of powerful new ideas. And, paradoxically, the list of reasons why an idea won't work often turns out to be incredibly useful as a design resource.

Do something

To get a sense of how prevalent the critic's conversation is in the world, think of a time when you were attempting to do something and people told you 'That will never work'.

Think of a time when you said it to someone else.

Look through a newspaper or listen to a current affairs programme and note all the instances where the whole tenor of the story is what's wrong and who's to blame.

Listen to conversations at work and listen for all the shoulds and shouldn'ts – these two words are how people express that they think something is wrong and someone is to blame.

Critics as designers

I started to appreciate the value of critics as designers when I was still at university. Like many budding scientists, I was inspired by the invention and innovation generated from Kennedy's bold commitment to putting a man on the moon before the decade was out. One of the staff members of the Chemistry Department at University College London, where I was studying, was involved in the creation of a new field of chemistry known as boron chemistry. I still remember him telling this story as he lectured us one morning.

As the space programme came to a successful conclusion with the first moon landing in 1969, the Chief Scientist apparently thanked all those experts who had told him it would never happen – particularly those who gave him a long list of reasons why not. He believed these people had done the designing for him.

A careful assessment of those lists gave him an almost complete blueprint for what he needed to create in order to deliver the programme. Rather than seeing it as a set of reasons why it would never work, he looked at them as a set of intelligent insights about things that were needed but not currently available.

One critic had told him that 'the space programme will never work because a fuel system with the right characteristics doesn't exist'. He went on to explain exactly what characteristics would be needed, laughingly dismissing the possibility that such a system could ever be created.

The reaction of the guy in charge surprised everyone: he gave someone the accountability to create a fuel system to the critic's exact specification. As a consequence, not only was a new form of chemistry invented, but the perfect fuel system emerged from it.

This story has been a constant inspiration to me. Every single one of my business ideas has provoked a 'That will never work' reaction from experts. In fact, I'm disappointed if my idea doesn't get that reaction now – that means it isn't powerful enough.

> *'Almost everyone said my idea wouldn't work. The idea of a 21-year-old knocking on the door of manufacturers with the intention of revolutionizing the optical industry didn't go down well. But this response only made me more determined. I set out to prove people wrong. I used my age and enthusiasm to my advantage and if someone said no, I went elsewhere.*
>
> *'Admittedly, at first, they were right. I was met with a wall of silence. Laboratories wouldn't talk to me, suppliers shook their heads and I couldn't even set up a business bank account or hire any office space. I wasn't short of negative responses or criticism, but I persevered and in each case I found a way round. After a bumpy ride I found a willing supplier and got the show on the road from my parent's garage. Just three years later and I have proved everyone wrong – we are the largest direct-seller of glasses in the world.'*

Jamie Murray Wells, founder of Glassesdirect.co.uk

The tyranny of the expert

So the first lesson for anyone trying to make a big idea happen is not to get disheartened if experts tell you it won't work. Do not be discouraged; most powerful new ideas get that reaction. Bill Gates' idea to put a PC on every desk and in every home didn't impress IBM, the experts in the field at the time. They thought the total world market for PCs would peak at less than 50,000.

When I was preparing a business plan for the mobile operator One2One (now T-Mobile), I asserted that the market for mobile phones in the UK could grow to 20 million users (it was about two million at the time). A consultant who was advising me actually told me not to be silly; it would peak at five million. It was a touch ironic that it was now me who was championing the mobile phone against critics. But this time I was right – the market did grow to 20 million and way beyond. This was largely driven by aggressive marketing strategies adopted by One2One and Orange that forced the established companies to respond with similar consumer-friendly pricing models.

'Every single one of them individually and collectively laughed in my face and said "You don't stand a chance".'

Cobra Beer founder Karan Bilimoria, talking about his first meetings in India when he had flown in to meet the management team of the largest independent brewery in the country

---

'I launched half a dozen magazines about a new fad called personal computing back in the 1980s, even though British magazine retailers and wholesalers at the time were unanimous in the belief that nobody would ever buy them. Those magazines have earned me tens of millions of pounds in the last 25 years.'

Felix Dennis, 2006

'I was told by experts "That will never work" about every big idea I've come up with. I was told that if cyclone technology was a good idea someone else would have done it already – but they hadn't even thought beyond bags.'

James Dyson

Why experts often dismiss new ideas out of hand

Experts often seem to be wedded to a set of beliefs and theories that they have been taught over many years and now accept without question. Experts on the whole are guardians of the status quo and cannot deal with an idea that breaches the current orthodoxy unless an authority in the field creates a whole new one for them. There's plenty of evidence that might just persuade you not to get discouraged if an expert dismisses your idea.

'We don't like their sound, and guitar music is on the way out.'

Decca executive rejecting The Beatles, 1962

'Man will never reach the moon, regardless of all the future scientific advances.'

Lee DeForest, inventor of vacuum tube/electronic valve, 1957

'Rail travel at high speed is not possible because passengers, unable to breathe, would die of asphyxia.'

Professor Dionysus Lardner, 1830

'Flight by machines heavier than air is impractical and insignificant, if not utterly impossible.'

Simon Newcomb, astronomer, 1902

'Such startling announcements as these should be deprecated as being unworthy of science and mischievous to its true progress.'

Sir William Siemens on Edison's announcement of the lightbulb, 1880

'I think there is a world market for maybe five computers.'

Thomas J. Watson Snr, IBM Chairman, 1943

Dealing with experts

Of course, experts are not always wrong in dismissing new ideas. In fact, more often than not, they are right. The reason for this is that most new ideas presented to them for evaluation are not well thought through or well-developed.

Professional venture capital investors do not dismiss new ideas out of hand. They are looking hard for the spark of genius that can create value out of nothing. So when they say that 90% of the new ideas they see have no chance of working, I listen with respect.

So here is my promise to you. If you follow my principles rigorously, your ideas and business plan will definitely be well thought through and well-developed. It will therefore have a good chance of success. If after all that you meet experts who say your idea won't work, you don't need to be discouraged. Deal with them like this:

1   Ignore them if they dismiss you or your idea out of hand. Think of them as Roosevelt's 'cold and timid souls'.
2   If after careful consideration they tell you it will never work, ask them to tell you exactly why, in as much detail as possible.
3   Keep searching for new critics who will give your idea careful thought and provide you with a long list of reasons why not.
4   Use these intelligent insights as an input to your design.

Using the Intelligent Insights

This is a tactic I've used consistently over the years. I use the list of reasons why something won't work (kindly provided to me by thoughtful experts) as a key input to my design. I call this list *the Intelligent Insights list*.

The concept of Firstdirect brought the critics out in full force. Even my own mother joined the masses of banking experts and strategy consultants in telling me what a bad idea it was. 'That's never going to work,' she said. 'You are wasting your time with that telephone banking nonsense. People hate using the telephone – they get passed from pillar to post, having to repeat the same story over and over again.'

Yes, that's true, I thought – but branches don't work for a lot of people either.

Her reaction inspired me to produce a number of statements of intention. These became the fundamental principles on which Firstdirect was founded and were at the heart of the exceptional service and customer loyalty that were built from the moment it launched:

- We will answer the phone within three rings.
- Customers will feel appreciated from the second the phone is answered.
- Our telephone associates will be empowered by training, by our rules and by our systems to take care of what the customer needs, even if the request is one we were not expecting or is beyond the normal call of duty.
- We will find a way to take care of anything a customer can do in a branch faster, cheaper and more conveniently.
- If a customer has to be transferred to another associate the customer information will be transferred with the call so they will not have to repeat themselves.

These statements put huge demands on every level of our business: recruitment and training, systems and processes, and product design. We had to go way beyond what other banks had attempted in most areas. For example, when a customer called, we had to produce a single view of all of their accounts instantaneously. This was in 1989 – some banks still can't do that today and it wasn't as if we had the luxury of building all of our systems from scratch. We used existing systems where we could – lots of different versions, all of which needed pulling together.

Six months after Firstdirect launched, an independent report concluded: 'Firstdirect consistently exceeds its customers' expectations.' Thanks Mum!

Fast-forward to Egg in 1998. We wanted to use the developing digital world to totally revolutionize the customers' experience of financial services. This set a whole army of critics' nerves on edge. The use of the Internet for banking provoked particular scorn from technology experts, strategy consultants and the CEOs of major banks. One critic likened using the Internet to being in a library where the books were scattered randomly on the floor with half of their pages missing, and where the lights kept going out.

This time it was my wife, Sue, who joined the opposition.

'The Internet!' she gasped. 'That'll never work. It's slow, unreliable and impersonal. I want somebody who knows what I want when I'm banking and can help me get it – what use is a dumb machine?'

'That's true,' I thought, 'but a lot of people hate managing their money with a bank looking over their shoulder. The telephone definitely has limitations in that respect – surely the interactivity of the Internet would be good for them.'

And that of course led to a series of statements of intention for Egg. We decided that dealing with Egg, whether by phone or over the Internet, would feel like dancing. We would be responsive to customers' every move and tailor our response. It would be a mass-market banking service tailored to the individual and would be about providing a stunning and individualized service to customers. We went on to define what we meant by 'stunning' and 'individualized' in some detail as a series of statements of intent:

- We will allow customers to tailor the features of all our products so their particular needs are met. (We eventually called these smart solutions.)

- We will allow customers to name their accounts with us rather than have them known by an account number.
- Customers can choose how they would like to be addressed by us (e.g. first name, Mrs Jones, etc.).
- We will tailor our telephone calls to both what the customer wants and their apparent emotional needs at the time they call, not to our targets for calls answered and call duration.
- We will help our customers decide what they need in savings, investments, loans and insurance, so that they can feel financially secure and supported.

As with Firstdirect, these statements of intent made huge demands on training, recruitment and system design. In this case (and particularly given the name), the demands on communication and brand were particularly intense. These demands provided the backbone of Egg's design and provoked much innovation. Egg achieved its five-year target for customer acquisition in just six months. It was a stunningly successful launch: it became the fastest-ever growing UK bank (according to the *FT*) and of course went on to become a successful and valuable business. Thanks Sue!

Egg and Firstdirect shared the same theory of how to make money: Great service at low cost, the service quality leading to high loyalty that itself leads to higher per-customer profitability than normal.

Egg not only attracted four million customers, it built a cool consumer brand in the process. In terms of illustrating the value of critics as a design resource, Egg is a perfect example.

You will find many entrepreneurs and innovators who will tell you, as I do, not to be discouraged by a 'That will never work' reaction from experts. However, you won't find that many who have proactively used all the negative reasons as Intelligent Insights to help their design. As I said before, it's one of the best-kept secrets in business.

When Richard Branson conceived of launching Virgin Direct to sell life insurance and investments by phone, and later over the Internet, the critics came out in force. Branson said:

> '*I have to admit that some healthy discussions took place about life insurance before we decided to launch Virgin Direct Life Insurance. Everyone snorted when they heard the idea – people hate life insurance. All the salesmen seem so corrupt, barging into your homes and taking secret commissions. It's a terrible industry.*'
> Richard Branson, 1998
>
> Branson took all of these Intelligent Insights and used them to design Virgin Direct in a way that would work. No salesmen, no hidden charges, simple index-linked products with low charges that everyone could understand – all wrapped up in the Virgin brand, which stood for being on the customers' side.
>
> In its first year (1995), Virgin Direct Private Equity Plan product was the most popular in the market.

> Peter Darbee is Chairman of the California-based energy utility Pacific Gas & Electric. His big idea is to create a carbon-neutral energy company and inspire the whole energy industry worldwide to follow his example.
>
> Peter told me:
>
> '*It is important to listen to the critics, understand what they have to say and judge for yourself whether it's valid or not. If it is valid, you will have to turn it into an opportunity. People condemn new ideas all the time. I encourage them to do that; but not only that, I also ask them to tell me exactly what problems they foresee and what ways they suggest of solving them. If they only see a problem, then I encourage them to express it as the set of things we need to solve to get the job done – then I ask what they are personally willing to do to help us find the solution.*'

I can promise you that using critics constructively to gain their Intelligent Insights works. It worked for the space programme, it's worked for Branson and Darbee, and it has worked for me time and time again.

Do something

So start right now. Create an initial Intelligent Insights list for your idea. Start the list yourself and then involve collaborators, friends and colleagues to add points. Write down all the reasons why your idea will never work, then talk about your idea to anyone you can get your hands on – particularly anyone with relevant expertise or anyone who might ultimately become a customer. If you are lucky enough to know an expert in the field or a strategy consultant, ask them. The object of this conversation is to get as many 'reasons why not' as possible in as much detail as possible.

Now go through the list using your judgment and intuition. Some of the reasons you are given will appear wrong or irrelevant to you. That's fine – back your judgment and ignore them. Pick the Intelligent Insights that seem particularly valid and important to you, and produce statements of intent that say what you are going to do to deal with the issues raised.

When you have turned the Intelligent Insights into 'statements of intent', you have used everything your critics have thrown at you (and your own doubts as well) to create a set of requirements that can drive your design and point you in exactly the right direction in order to be successful.

4

Making million-pound ideas

'The way to get good ideas is to get lots of ideas and throw the bad ones away.'

Linus Pauling, American chemist and Nobel Prize winner

The key to coming up with good ideas, as Pauling says, is to come up with lots and simply discard the bad ones. This chapter not only tackles the issue of how to generate countless ideas, but how to differentiate the gold from the grit and get rid of the latter.

It's definitely worth you reading on, even if you already have a firm view of the big idea you want to implement. Even if you end up with exactly the same idea, I believe there will be fundamental differences that will stack the odds in your favour. Not only is your idea likely to be stronger, but you will be much better equipped in the art of explaining it to others.

Customer insight

Customer insight refers to the discovery of new information about how customers lead their lives at home and at work along with what motivates them. It is the discovery of what works well for people and what's not working at all. In essence, we are looking for unsolved problems that our products and services could rectify. Customer insight is therefore truly invaluable when it comes to both generating and evaluating ideas.

I started to learn about customer insight 20 years ago when I took on the creation of Firstdirect. Rupert Howell, the co-founder of the advertising agency HHCL, worked with me on this aspect of the business at the time. He taught me a lot about the subject in all its complexities. He began by busting a common myth:

> *'Maslow's hierarchy of needs is a good structure for thinking about what drives customers. At the basic level you have lust, hunger and protection. This explains why you hear a lot of people talk about marketing as just about sex, greed and fear, but these drives soon get sated in western society leaving you to address the higher levels of need such as reputation, status and identity. We want goods and services to satisfy our basic needs, but we also want them to say something positive about us.'*

Over the years since that conversation I've been an enthusiastic student and practitioner in the art of marketing. I've learnt a wealth of priceless lessons about how to use customer insight to formulate the kinds of ideas that spell success. And thankfully for all those like me who believe we can rise above our basic instincts, I've discovered Rupert was right – there is more to human motivation and marketing than fear, greed and sex.

There are essentially two disciplines in marketing:

1   Customer insight (which I cover in this chapter):
    – determining customer needs and coming up with
      ideas for new products
    – turning ideas into fully designed products fit for im-
      plementation and launch
    – determining the number and type of customers (busi-
      ness or consumer) who might buy a particular prod-
      uct.
2   Communications (which I cover in Chapter 7) – brand-
    ing, advertising, direct marketing and promotion.

How leading companies use customer insight

One method of customer insight you might be familiar with is
focus groups. A focus group involves an invited group of participants sharing their thoughts, feelings, attitudes and ideas on a
certain subject. Governments and large companies often employ
them to try and determine exactly what people want, think they
want or simply think. Focus groups have their place: while they
can be very good at getting people to share and talk through
their issues and opinions, using them to ask people what they
want is not a good idea. Ironic as it sounds, you can't determine
customer needs by simply asking people.

*'If I'd asked my customers what they wanted, they'd have said a
faster horse.'*

Henry Ford

So what do you do instead? Well, leaders in this field use a multi-
stage process. I'm going to describe this in detail, even though it
is likely to be well beyond your means at this stage. It's worth understanding this professional approach because later I'm going

to give you a simplified version that should be well within your budget.

Many leading companies take the following steps when it comes to determining human needs. The example I use concentrates on the needs of people as consumers, but the same principles apply when looking at the needs of people at work:

1   Observe people in action in both their homes and at work, and talk to them individually. For example, if I wanted to know how people were using banking products, I'd have professionals observe their behaviour in a branch, question them about what they were trying to get done when they visited a branch and ask how the whole experience worked for them. These customers would subsequently be visited at home, where they would be asked to demonstrate how they managed their money and how they viewed banking as a service. This could even be in abstract terms such as drawing a picture – a mental representation of the way they see their money and the way they manage it.

2   These observations are analysed, looking out for things that aren't working and things that are missing from the products and services they are currently using. For example, where banking is concerned, you might conclude that there are no products that allow customers to visualize money exactly the way they think about it.

3   Brainstorm lots of ideas for new solutions to the problems and issues you have observed in step 2.

4   Decide on any solutions you want to develop further and come up with a hypothesis for the target market. You are normally specifying a particular segment of the population based on age, employment, salary, location, interests and attitude (or particular types of business).

5 Produce a description or demonstration of a solution and try it out one-to-one with a relatively small number of people (no more than 16). Modify your design according to the feedback or throw it away and start again.

6 Produce a prototype of the solution after you have modified it to take into account what you learnt in step 5. A prototype is basically something that consumers can see and experience (e.g. a working website, a drawing of a new retail concept, an early hand-built version of an electronic product such as an iPod or even a pre-production model of a new car).

7 Convene a focus group of eight to ten people to find out what they think about the prototype and why. If you do enough focus groups, speaking to 60–100 people, you can make a good guess at the total number of people who would be interested in your product and what they are prepared to pay for it. It's a calculation that goes something like this:

   – About 20% of the people we spoke to looked interested enough to pay us £10 a month.
   – The total number of people in our target market is five million. This is done by specifying the types of customers who are likely to be interested in your product (e.g. by age, sex, lifestyle and attitude) and using one of the many marketing databases (type 'marketing resources' into an Internet search engine), which tell you how many people of that demographic are living in the geographical area you are interested in.
   – Therefore we will appeal to 1m people.
   – We should aim at 30% of those people in three years, i.e. our target is 300,000 people over three years. Thirty per cent penetration of a target market is a good rule of thumb for planning purposes.

Quantitative research

Finally, I'll mention for completeness a form of customer insight that big companies often engage in – quantitative research. This involves asking 1000–5000 people a set of simple questions about their likelihood of buying your product. This is often done in the form of a questionnaire over the phone, the Internet or in person. You are trying to get a statistically valid view of the number of people who are likely to buy your product rather than just a rough estimate. However, this is almost never done for an innovative new product or service, because it takes too long to explain the details to enough people to get a statistically valid result.

> *'Beware of conventional quantitative research. Whilst it can give you the norm and tell you how many people do or think something it won't tell you the most important thing – why they do it. It fails to pick up on any of the mental intricacies you need.'*

> Mark Ratcliff, founder of market research agency Murmur

The power of passion

Entrepreneurs have a great advantage over big companies. Entrepreneurs build products they are passionate about, not just those that will make money. Entrepreneurs, as we will see later, often identify new products just by thinking about their own needs as a consumer, their own experience of an industry or their knowledge of a technology.

If we could combine this passion and experience-based insight with some aspects of the professional process I have just described, we would have a potent mix indeed – a real edge.

That's what the techniques I'm going to describe are all about. I have adapted some professional techniques and created a simplified, low-cost process that you can use as a powerful supplement to your existing knowledge and intuition. Let's start by deepening your understanding of customer insight in terms of generating your big idea.

Ideas that work

Ideas that work meet an unmet need – they provide a solution to something that people or businesses need now or might need in the future. This need might be currently unmet because it has not yet been recognized. If this need has been met, you might well develop a cheaper, faster or more convenient solution than the one available.

Firstdirect's telephone banking service met a need for access to banks 24 hours a day, seven days a week. It was perfect for people whose location, work or family commitments made visiting a branch in normal opening hours difficult. It also appealed to those who could visit branches but hated queuing or who found staff unable or unwilling to provide the service they desired.

The Egg card allowed people to shop safely and easily online. As well as conventional credit card services, it also offered a better interest rate and more convenience than its branch-based competitors.

Google met a need for finding literally anything on the Internet in less than a second. Search engines existed before Google but none were as comprehensive, as fast or as easy to use.

Needs can be divided into two basic categories – functional and emotional:

> • Functional needs are met by what the product actually does.
> • Emotional needs are centred on the desire to feel or look a certain way – attractive, successful, connected, sexy, secure, stylish, smart and so on.

The point I really want to emphasize is that designing a product for consumers or businesses involves constructing a user experience that works at both a functional and emotional level.

One product that achieves this brilliantly is the iPod. Digital music existed before the iPod but Apple made the whole experience easy, stylish and highly desirable. The iPod met a bunch of emotional needs as well as functional ones. In functional terms it was easy to use and made managing and transporting a large digital music collection incredibly simple. It met emotional needs in terms of its stylish design and desirability.

'As a design team, I cannot remember the last time where we were collectively lusting after a product as badly as after an iPod.'

Jonathan Ive, iPod designer and internationally renowned winner of the London Design Museum's Designer of the Year Award in 2002 and 2003

———————

'People think it's this veneer, that the designers are handed this box and told, "Make it look good!". That's not what we think design is. It's not just what it looks like and feels like. Design is how it works.'

Steve Jobs (from Walker, 2003)

———————

Do something

The Internet provided the impetus for an explosion of innovative ideas. It is a wonderfully Darwinian platform on which numerous theories about unmet needs, both functional and emotional, are tested to destruction.

Try making a list of all the things that the Internet has enabled you to do (or experience) better, faster, cheaper or with higher quality than before. Are there any needs (functional and emotional) that were completely unmet before?

Think about your needs as a consumer and your needs at work.

Market research reports consistently state that, for the average Internet user, Google is literally 'loved' – a fantastic response and one that should frighten the life out of actual and potential competitors. What emotional needs is Google meeting to achieve that response?

The point of these questions is to deepen your sensitivity to customer needs. Once you have done this, you can embark on your own search for ideas that work or validate and strengthen the ideas you already have.

Searching for ideas that work

Remember, a great idea doesn't have to be your own. Firstdirect wasn't really my idea. It emerged organically from a team conversation about telephone banking initiated by a young Midland Bank executive named Steve Mayers who had seen what was happening with telephone banking in the USA. I saw its potential, stretched it, infected others with my own enthusiasm and made it happen.

Mercury already had a fledgling consumer division along-side its core business-to-business services when I got there. My contribution was to see the potential of the consumer market and infect others with my enthusiasm so we were able to get a great team and the right resources.

Egg also emerged organically from numerous team conversations about the future of banking in the digital world. I simply harnessed its potential and got the show on the road.

It's the same with Garlik – the idea doesn't belong to one individual. It emerged from numerous conversations among the team. In this case it was Garlik's CEO Tom Ilube who saw its potential and made sure it was implemented fantastically well.

Initially, what's really important is your ability to see the potential of an idea so that you can grab it and stretch it into something that maximizes its value.

You can start looking for ideas in one of three places:

1   An industry you know well (e.g. banking, technology, retailing, consulting, publishing, travel, etc.). Ask yourself how customers (businesses or consumers) could be better served by that industry both now and in the future.

2   Yourself as a consumer. What products and services are you unsatisfied with because they don't really meet your needs? Are there any products or services that don't exist and that you would love to be able to buy?

3   An emerging technology that you know well. Ask yourself how this could be used in the future to better serve customers (businesses or consumers).

Starting with an industry

'Many entrepreneurs start out because they have seen something that customers need that the company they are working for can't or won't provide.'

Tim Brown, CEO of design and innovation consultancy
Ideo

Many new ideas that end up as big companies start out this way. This was certainly the case with Firstdirect. We started with banking, an industry we knew well, and we looked at its limitations – inconvenient opening hours, queues and variable quality of service in branches. As far as banking as a business was concerned, the branch network was very costly to run. Therefore, by swapping branches for telephones, we knew we could provide better service at lower cost.

Celtel, the mobile phone company that developed franchises all over Africa, was built by people already working in the telecommunications industry. They realized the need to build and operate a communications network to deliver reliable and competitive services in Africa. Mobile telephony was the only plausible way to do it – it would have been too expensive and slow to put fixed-line telephony in place.

One of the most successful Silicon Valley start-ups of recent times was created by the former Oracle executive, Mark Benioff. Oracle, founded by Larry Ellison in 1977, is one of the world's largest software businesses, employing more than 50,000 people and supplying companies all over the world with database management systems and many other types of enterprise software. Mark knew the software industry inside out. He spotted a gap in the market when he realized that many companies couldn't afford or didn't want to invest in expensive in-house computer systems to manage their sales forces. Mark started Salesforce. com, which provides affordable Web-based sales management systems to small and large companies alike.

Another exemplary company that spotted a niche is My Family Care, which won *The Daily Telegraph*/CPP innovation competition in 2007. It was founded by Ben Black, who knew the childcare business inside out, and Venetia Wickham, who had a background in computer dating. Their combined expertise created a company that met a clear need using a resource that few others knew existed.

> *'My big idea was to allow parents to book childcare online and to allow employers to subsidize the costs for their employees. Parents with young children have a childcare 'breakdown' about nine times a year. Typically their nanny, au pair or childminder will be ill, on holiday or have their own emergency, or the child might be at nursery and have a minor cold or conjunctivitis. It's stressful all round. There is pressure to go to work and the old 'family and friends' network is not what they used to be.*

> *'Due to the expansion of childcare facilities, there are many unoccupied nursery places on any particular day and due to an influx of trained staff from eastern Europe, there is currently an excess of nannies too.*

> *'My Family Care uses computer dating techniques to match parents in need with instantly available care. As well as the childcare provision, the business is also offering homecare directed at people with jobs also looking after older relatives.*

> *'I already knew that there was an excess supply of labour in the childcare market. So the challenge was to build a platform that allowed parents to book the childcare they wanted (nannies, nurseries, childminders) in one easy process, either online or via*

a call centre. Lots of people had tried doing something similar, i.e. offering back-up childcare. But I knew that to be successful, the service could not rely on someone making a phone call to see if childcare was available. It's a heavily regulated industry with lots of sensitivities, so it was much more of a challenge than I originally thought.'

Ben Black, co-founder of My Family Care

Starting with yourself as a consumer

Innocent Drinks produces smoothies that are sold in supermarkets and coffee shops in the UK, the Republic of Ireland, Holland, France, Belgium and Denmark. Innocent dominates the UK smoothie market and employs 280 people.

Co-founder Richard Reed told me:

'Innocent started with a vision shared by three ex-university friends: myself, Adam Balon and John Wright. Our vision was: "Let's find something that makes life a little bit easier and a little bit better."

'We've always found that there's something about modern living that makes it hard to be healthy. That's why we gave up our jobs over five years ago and started making smoothies. We wanted people to think of Innocent Drinks as their one healthy habit – like going to the gym, but without the communal shower afterwards.

'We went on a snowboarding weekend in February 1998 and said to ourselves when we come back we'll make it happen.'

By August 1998, Innocent was selling its first smoothies from a stall at a music festival in London. Their products hit the shops by April 1999.

Cobra Beer was founded by Karan Bilimoria. He was 27 and £20,000 in debt when he noticed a gaping hole in the market for his unique vision. With no prior knowledge of the marketplace, Karan Bilimoria took on the established giants of the industry and won.

'I saw that the market was dominated by harsh, gassy Eurofizz beers, all poor partners to food, and so I wanted to produce a premium, high-quality lager which would complement rather than fight against food. I had a big vision – to brew the finest ever Indian beer and to make it a global beer brand.'

Karan Bilimoria, 2007

When it came to renewing his glasses prescription while studying for his finals at university, Jamie Murray Wells was astonished by the hefty price tags that the high street chains were charging.

'It's just a bit of wire – there's more metal in a teaspoon,' he says. 'Glasses can't be worth that much. It seemed to me that there must be a huge discrepancy between the real value and what was on sale in the shops.'

After some market research, Jamie discovered that the manufacturing process was largely automated. Designer glasses cost less than £10 to produce. He decided to change all that, revolutionizing the entire industry in the process.

On 1 July 2004, at the age of 21 and with no formal business training, Jamie launched Glassesdirect.co.uk into an industry dominated by four major optical chains. Three years later and his successful business, selling cut-price prescription glasses over the Internet, was the largest direct seller of glasses in the world, selling a pair every seven minutes.

Virgin is famous for creating new products by putting themselves in customers' shoes. Will Whitehorn, now President of Virgin Galactica, told me about the design of the award winning service on Virgin Atlantic:

'For Richard, airlines weren't about engineering. He looked at it as a consumer. For him, flying on a plane for eight hours was an eight-hour retail experience. He revolutionized aviation around concepts of fun and entertainment. Customers don't care about technology or logistics, they care about feeling good and having fun.'

Starting with an emerging technology

My new company Garlik started with an emerging technology. This technology allows us to merge Web information with other publicly available sources of data such as the electoral roll or credit registers, for example. Key pieces of information like names, dates, companies and telephone numbers can be extracted and stored in a huge database for processing and querying. It has numerous applications but the one we focused on initially was allowing an individual to find all the publicly available information about them and to keep track of any changes. This meets two otherwise unmet needs: protection against identity theft and the ability to monitor and manage your reputation. This grows increasingly important as potential employers or business partners turn to online sources of reference.

Egg also focused on what emerging technology could do for customers. At our launch we made it clear that Egg was the first bank specifically designed for the digital age. Egg would use this technology to transform customers' experience of financial services, giving them solutions to all of their money needs.

By starting with emerging technology, we were in good company. Google created a new and smarter technology for Web searches and built from there.

> 'There is so much leverage in science and technology – I think most people don't realize that. There is so much that can be done with these new technologies. We are an example of that.'

Larry Page, co-founder of Google

And when I look at Apple, I always think about how stylish and easy to use they can make new technologies.

> 'Apple's core strength is to bring very high technology to mere mortals in a way that surprises and then delights them and that they can figure out how to use.'

Steve Jobs, 2005

It's all about unmet needs

Wherever you start – whether it's with an industry you think could do better, a product you would love to buy if only it existed or with an emerging technology you are excited about – you have to end up with products and services that meet a currently unmet need.

In giving you a process to generate and evaluate many potential million-dollar ideas, I'm going to suggest using a combination of your own knowledge and interests together with a simplified version of a professional insight process, similar to the one used by Ideo.

Back in 1995, I visited the San Francisco offices of Ideo, the leading design and innovation consultancy. It was located in an old fish warehouse on the waterfront. Creativity and innovation permeate every corner of this building – just visiting is an exhilarating experience. Since then I have undertaken a number of projects with Ideo and I've truly learnt to appreciate the value of what they do.

Ideo's speciality is uncovering human needs – needs that individuals may not yet be able to articulate for themselves. They are famous for observing customers' behaviour and putting themselves in the customers' shoes to experience what they experience. In undertaking a redesign of the emergency room at the Depaul clinic in Missouri, an Ideo designer once pretended to need help and experienced the whole process of admission through treatment to discharge, managing to videotape the entire thing.

Ideo's overall approach is designed to determine unmet needs. It consists of the following steps:

1 Understand the market and what the client wants.
2 Observe real people in real-life situations.
3 Brainstorm and visualize possible new products and the people who will use them through computer simulation or prototypes.
4 Evaluate and refine the prototypes with input from anyone who might have anything useful to say, as well as potential customers in one-to-one interviews.
5 Implement.

As CEO Tim Brown told me: 'You must uncover human needs in order to design compelling user value propositions. Otherwise, why would anyone want to buy what you have to sell?'

I'm going to describe two processes that do just that, allowing you to use your own knowledge, experience and interests to harness some of the power of Ideo's professional idea-generation process both easily and cheaply.

> The first process will help you to generate up to 100 ideas and pick what looks like a winner. The second process enables you to test and strengthen your idea. These processes are not only good for finding your initial big idea; they can be used again and again as your business develops to come up with new products and services for your customers.

Process 1: Idea-generation

Step 1

Get a small number of people together in a relaxed environment for a couple of hours. All you need is a room, notepads and pens, Post-it notes, and a wall, a board or a large piece of paper to stick them on.

Step 2

Either: Start with an industry you personally know well. Ask everyone to write down as many ideas as possible for ways that customers (businesses or consumers) could be better served by that industry. Have everyone write down their own ideas, each one on a separate Post-it note, and keep going until everyone has run out of steam.

Or: Start with yourselves as consumers. Ask everyone to write down as many ideas as possible for products and services that don't exist but that you feel could serve a need. Have everyone write down their own ideas, each one on a separate Post-it note, and keep going until everyone has run out of steam.

Or: Start with an emerging technology that you personally know well. Be sure everyone understands your enthusiasm and vision for the technology, and ask everyone to write down as many ideas as possible for ways in which it could be used in the future to serve businesses or consumers. Have everyone write down their own ideas, each one on a separate Post-it note, and keep going until everyone has run out of steam.

Step 3

Take a break. Get people to go out to a shopping centre or anywhere they consider relevant and appropriate, maybe in pairs. Just wander around and observe people in action. Think about your product idea when you are out. It's not professional observation in action, but it's remarkable how it can trigger new thoughts.

Step 4

When people have returned, ask them to review their previous ideas. Get rid of some, change some, add some more.

Ask people to read out their ideas one at a time before sticking them on the wall.

If two ideas are similar, make sure they are placed together. You will probably find that the individual ideas will cluster into five to ten big ideas, with a few outliers that you just discard.

Now take charge. Write each big idea (i.e. the ones you have derived from the clustering of individual ideas) on a new piece of paper. It's completely up to you how you do this.

Next ask everybody to mark each big idea out of ten. They should keep the marks to themselves at this time. The higher the mark, the more powerful they think the idea is.

Take each big idea one at a time and ask each person to read out their mark and give their reasons for it. Listen to the reasons, not the mark.

Add up the marks and then choose the idea you want to take further. It need not be the one with the highest marks – the point of marking is just to get people to talk about the ideas. Don't try for consensus or agreement among the group. Consensus is usually reached by eliminating everything that anybody doesn't like – this reduces the power of an idea rapidly. You retain power by having one person accountable for the final decision after they have listened to what everybody has to say. There can only be one leader when putting a new idea into the world – and that's you. It's your decision, so make it based on your personal intuition and enthusiasm.

Process 2: Getting a reaction

This is one way to test out the strength of an idea. Your intention here is not to get an answer to the question 'Does this idea work?' You are still in generative mode – i.e. you are looking for ways to amend and strengthen the idea so that it has the best possible chance of working.

Step 1

Write about your idea in the style of a full page advert in a national newspaper. It should aim to persuade people to buy or use the product or service that you are thinking of creating.

Take a look at a few newspaper ads in the personal finance and property sections just to get an idea.

For example, if I were to have done this for Firstdirect it would have been:

Banking at your convenience

Today saw the launch of a new bank called Firstdirect. We are dedicated to giving you great service by telephone 24 hours a day, seven days a week.

Why not give us a try and open an account? There's no need to close your existing account until you are completely comfortable – but it may reassure you to know that we are owned by Midland Bank, which means your money is safe, although we are a completely separate organization.

You can open an account by phone – just call 0800 100 100 anytime.

You will get the best rate of interest available in the UK on your credit balances and easy access to an overdraft should you need it.

You will receive a cheque book, a cheque card and a credit card, and you will be able to withdraw money from more than 3000 ATMs.

It's easy to pay in, too. You can do this by post or over the counter at any Midland Bank branch.

We don't have any branches of our own – we don't need them. If you need anything, you can telephone us any time at your convenience, 24 hours a day, 365 days a year. No more visiting branches, no more queues.

Once you have a Firstdirect account then a personal loan, a mortgage, foreign currency, savings accounts and bill payments, and any advice, help or troubleshooting you need is available just by picking up the telephone.

We answer all calls within three rings and our staff are all highly trained, intelligent professionals dedicated to giving you exactly what you need.

As you can see, it doesn't have to be perfect. It's not intended to be a real advert; it's what we call a *stimulus*.

If you have anything else that illustrates your idea (drawings, samples, a scale model, photos, video clips or a prototype website), then use them too. None of these are essential, but the more you have, the more useful you will find the process – particularly if the idea is very innovative and people might have problems picturing it.

Step 2

You need to locate about 16 people, none of whom took part in your idea generation. More than half should be people you think may be interested in buying the product or service, either for themselves or for the businesses they work for. The others should be a mixture of potential critics and creative, articulate people – you never know, they just might be in your market, and their thoughts are invaluable.

You'll need between 30 minutes and an hour, one-to-one, with each person. Once again, obviously it can be quite a challenge to recruit these people. You will have to use friends, friends of friends, friends of family, people you work with, people you know in other businesses, their friends/contacts, etc. But it's a trivial problem compared to those you will face later in making your idea real, so don't be daunted or give up.

> 'I'm a big believer in talking to opinion-formers. These are people who can talk knowledgably about a subject or product but still represent the population at large. For example, we were recruited by a condom manufacturer to research the market for new product innovations and ideas. We spoke with therapists, sex shops and high-class prostitutes. It wasn't the easiest re-

search route – understandably, people were often suspicious and unwilling to open up at first, but it was worth all the effort. Our interviewees gave us some amazing insights and new angles (if you'll pardon the pun) that have contributed to launching many successful new products.'

Mark Ratcliff, founder of market research agency
Murmur

Step 3

In each interview, let the person read your stimulus. Show them any other illustrative material you have. Ask them the following:

> • What is your opinion of the product and why?
> • What benefits do you see in the product and why?
> • What features do you like and why?
> • What features do you like least and why?
> • What other features would you like to see and why?
> • What problems do you foresee with this product and why?
> • What would stop you using this product and why?
> • What sort of people do you think would be interested in this product and why?
> • Would you use this product and if so, why?

Make sure you capture their answers, either by writing notes or by recording them.

With each question, keep probing for needs and motivations. Keep exploring why your participants are saying what they are saying. When they give you a reason for their opinion, ask them why it is important to them. Keep going on each question until the person has nothing more to say.

Step 4: Drawing conclusions

Sit down, preferably with at least some of the group who generated the idea with you in the first place, and go through the results of the interviews.

Remember, you are not interested in how many people said they would use the product. It is still in the design stage – how many people will use it comes later, once you have a final product.

A lot of big ideas get the thumbs-down in early research, the Sony Walkman being a famous example. Firstdirect didn't fare too well in early research either. People could only get their minds around telephone banking when they could use it.

> *'When it came to consumer research, Al and Monkey for ITV Digital advertising campaign didn't fare too well. In fact people were appalled. It was called downmarket, cheap and a turnoff, but it still turned out to be a huge hit ... sometimes you might just be listening to the wrong people.'*

Mark Ratcliff, founder of market research agency
Murmur

What you are listening for in all the interviews is how important people see the unmet needs that you are seeking to address. You might also discover new unmet needs or insights that you can use to strengthen your idea. So stay alert for emerging needs, i.e. those that aren't yet obvious but that people can see developing along with new technology or social trends.

For example, we could deduce from early research on First-direct that there was a definite unmet need for people to bank without having to visit branches. Branches were really disliked for their limiting opening hours, inconvenient locations, queues and patchy service. As people got busier and banks closed more and more branches, this need was likely to grow. People didn't necessarily buy telephone banking as a solution because they didn't understand it, but we could at least be certain there was a real functional need.

Early research also told us that some emotional needs could be better met by Firstdirect than by existing banks, e.g. feeling in control, intelligent, recognized and supported. We hadn't realized this before and it shaped both our approach to marketing and some aspects of our customer service.

So the key question is: does your idea have the possibility to meet enough unmet functional and emotional needs now or in the future to make it a winner?

Once you've done your research it's a case of using your intuition.

If your answer is 'no', go back to the idea-generation process and pick another idea to test. Persistence and an unwillingness to be beaten are key features of successful people, so keep going until you get to 'yes'.

I'm not going to suggest you use conventional focus groups to check out your final design. This method is likely to be too expensive and laborious to do professionally right now and it's no job for an amateur. You can use focus groups later, if you like, when you have enough money. For now you are going to have to use your judgment.

Do something

Practise some idea-generation and customer insight. This will also help you check out and strengthen any ideas you might already have. If you don't really have a business idea yet, you can use this process to find one.

I want you to run a meeting that aims to generate at least 100 new ideas to meet unmet needs using Process 1, which I described in this Chapter. An ideal number of people for such a meeting is six to ten, but you can do it with as few as two or three. Don't do it alone. Beg, plead, persuade and bribe but get together a bunch of people who are willing to help you – friends, family, co-workers, anybody you can get your hands on. The most valuable people will be those who may eventually end up working with you, but anyone can make a contribution. Older children (11 plus, depending on the product) can be absolutely fantastic to use in such groups – they have an unrivalled natural honesty and creativity.

Start by asking everyone to share their thoughts about the needs that the Internet has fulfilled. If you don't have children present, feel free to raise sex, fear and greed at this point. It normally gets everyone laughing and more relaxed.

Then go through all of the steps of Process 1 exactly as I have described. Pick one of the ideas you came up with and go through all the steps of Process 2. Just try the idea out on a handful of friends at this stage – you are just familiarizing yourself with the approach.

When you come to set up a business for real, use Process 1 intensively with the key members of your team to come up with ideas or strengthen existing ones, and use Process 2 to check out all ideas with potential users exactly as I described earlier.

A quick word on patents

While we are talking about ideas, it's worth addressing the issue of patents. A patent is a set of exclusive rights granted to an inventor for a fixed period of time. It precludes anyone else from copying the invention and is thus some protection against competition.

Notably, you can't patent an idea – only its implementation. For example, Viagra is patented by Pfizer – but the actual idea of a drug to cure erectile dysfunction can't be patented. Therefore, different implementations of the same idea, such as Cialis from Lilly, can emerge as competitors.

If your idea involves very novel technology or a very novel implementation of a business process, you may be able to patent the implementation. If this is a possibility, you should make that clear in your financial plan (see Chapter 5).

If you think you have a patentable implementation, take professional advice early. You need to keep copious records. Don't rely on patents to deter imitators, but they can raise the bar for competition and provide a revenue source for licensing.

One thing you must do is avoid breaching someone else's patent or infringing their intellectual property. If you think this is a possibility, seek professional advice – search the Internet for 'patent lawyers'.

Back to customer insight

You should now be able to articulate your idea, along with the unmet functional and emotional needs it meets or might meet in the future, and the sort of people who might buy it.

That's a great place to be!

5

Find funding

'Nearly every man who develops an idea works it up to the point where it looks impossible, and then he gets discouraged. That's not the place to become discouraged.'

Thomas Edison

———————

Once you are clear about your proposition, the next step is to think about how you will fund its development. In order to do this you will need to put together a financial plan. This is normally the point when doubts creep in and it all starts to feel too difficult. This is definitely not the time to get discouraged – if you are feeling a bit frightened, that's actually a good thing. It means you have what I call a *Goldilocks idea* – neither too hot nor too cold.

If your idea is too hot (that is, far too difficult and challenging to implement), you won't feel frightened because you know there is no realistic prospect of getting it done. It will remain a dream because that's a safe place to be.

On the other hand, if the idea is too cold (that is, far too easy to implement), you won't be frightened either. You know it won't really change anything for you or anyone else, and you probably won't bother.

To be just right, the idea needs to feel at least a little bit impossible – impossible for you, right now, given your situation and your resources. But beneath that feeling of impossibility, you still have an uncanny belief that somehow you could pull this off. You are simultaneously excited and frightened. You go to bed thinking 'I'm going to do this' and wake up thinking 'I must be out of my mind'. Just thinking about it makes your palms sweaty, but you can't help getting excited and enthusiastic. Well, congratulations – that's exactly where you should be right now. It's perfect.

This is the way I've felt before committing myself to everything I've ever done. I've learned to love the electric feeling that falls somewhere between excitement and fear – I know it means I'm on to a potential winner. So please, please, *please* – if you feel this way, don't be discouraged and don't give up.

If you don't feel this way, then there are two possible reasons why. Either you haven't worked the idea up to the point at which it starts to scare you just a little – in this case, go back and do some more stretching (Chapter 4). Or if your idea is just too tough for you to take on, then dampen it down a bit using the techniques below.

- Make a list of any simplifying assumptions you can think of. These are things that cut down the scope of what you are taking on without destroying it completely.
- A simplifying assumption will normally involve:
  - giving yourself more time to implement the idea – assuming you have enough money to do this (time is definitely money in this case)
  - restricting the idea to a certain customer group or a certain geographical location initially
  - reducing dependence on novel technology

- – reducing the number of products and services you
    set out to implement initially.
- Play with the simplifying assumptions until you end up
    with an idea that feels just right.

At Egg we initially intended to launch with a full range of investment, banking and insurance products, as well as an investment
advice service. When we began to consider the practicalities,
it became obvious that we had to simplify things to have any
chance of success. So we cut the initial product range right down
to a savings account, a mortgage and a personal loan. It still gave
us enough scope to demonstrate what Egg was all about without
giving us a totally impossible challenge.

When we were looking at the possibility of launching Egg in
the USA, we reduced the scope of what felt like a completely un-
manageable problem by concentrating on what it would take to
launch Egg in just one area, one where the idea of Egg was very
appealing to many people who lived there. Our research showed
this to be Los Angeles.

Now assuming you have a Goldilocks idea, what you need to
do next is concentrate on securing some money to implement it.
That probably feels like a pretty bold commitment at this stage.

Bold commitments

Before you think too much about that, let me remind you of one
of the key lessons in Chapter 1. It's about boldness.

Do you remember the Goethe quote? It was the inspiration
that got me going on Firstdirect:

> *'Whatever you can do or dream you can, begin it. Boldness has
> genius, power and magic in it. Begin it now.'*

Johann Wolfgang von Goethe

Years after I first came across that quote, I was handed a piece of paper by a change consultant at a seminar I was attending. It read:

> *'Until one is committed there is hesitancy, the chance to draw back, always ineffectiveness. Concerning all acts of initiative (and creation) there is one elementary truth, the ignorance of which kills countless ideas and splendid plans: that the moment one definitely commits oneself, then Providence moves too. All sorts of things occur to help one that would never otherwise have occurred. A whole stream of events issues from the decision, raising in one's favour all manner of unforeseen incidents and meetings and material assistance which no man could have dreamt would have come his way. I have learned a deep respect for one of Goethe's couplets: "Whatever you can do, or dream you can, begin it. Boldness has genius, power and magic in it."'*

W.H. Murray, Scottish mountaineer, 1951

Murray articulates the power of bold commitment, not just bold beginnings. In my experience, much of what he says actually happens – as long as you continually reinforce your commitment through your enthusiasm. Your enthusiasm becomes magnetic, attracting people who find that it resonates with them. The people you attract bring resources, assistance, contacts, ideas – it feels like magic, but there's no mystery really. Genuine commitment to an enthusiastically communicated big idea is a great attractor – it always has been.

> *'When you meet someone full of enthusiasm for an idea, I'm not sure whether people have the heart to tell you what they are really thinking. I managed to get two important players in the*

*childcare industry involved – Asquith, the country's leading
chain of nurseries, and a company called Accor Services, which
provides childcare vouchers with my sheer enthusiasm.'*

Ben Black, co-founder of My Family Care

I've heard many people say you have to be lucky to succeed in business, but I believe that much of what people refer to as 'luck' is actually the W.H. Murray effect. It would be more accurate to say 'you have to be genuinely committed and enthusiastic' to succeed in business.

So let's use some of that genuine commitment and enthusiasm to give us the energy to think about a subject that always gives people the shivers: the practical task of producing a financial plan and raising some money.

Getting funded: the growth route

I would like to urge you to you to read this carefully, not to skip through it. It is information I wish I'd had 20 years ago. It would have made millions of pounds' worth of difference to me, as well as making my business life a lot smoother.

I have my own particular view about the best funding route that is appropriate for most new businesses. It's the route we took with Garlik. I call it *the growth route*.

The growth route refers to using your own resources at first, but bringing in external funding as soon as possible in order to maximize the growth potential and value of your business. As the name suggests, the idea is to grow the company as fast as possible.

1. Developing the concept

You will always have to do a certain amount of work using your own resources, no matter how limited they may be. Often what you are investing is merely your spare time. Sometimes you will need to use personal savings or family money, if it is available. This funding method is known as bootstrapping.

Before you can think about bringing in external funding you need to:

- Produce a financial plan and a powerful sales pitch. (I'll show you how to do both of these later in this chapter.)
- Produce a prototype, model or demonstration of the product you are intending to build. At minimum this might be the stimulus material you used to test out your product idea with potential customers as I described in the last chapter. Depending on how credible your plan is, you might need to build a working prototype before professionals will consider funding your idea.
- Hire an accountant to help you form a limited company. You will need to take your accountant's advice on all of the rules and regulations about raising money from external investors.

You may be able to continue funding the company yourself until it becomes self-funding. If you can't continue to fund the company yourself, or choose not to, then once you have completed Stage 1 you need to bring in external investors to provide enough cash to take the business forward.

2. Bring in the angels

There is a whole industry out there looking for big ideas to invest in. It's called the venture capitalist (VC) industry. The European industry alone invests more than €1bn per quarter from funds operated by VC companies such as Doughty Hanson, 3i, Index, Benchmark, Apax and numerous others. These are tough, rational people who support entrepreneurs with large sums of money, are actively engaged on the boards of companies and strongly influence their strategic directions.

Getting VCs to invest in your business is a very formal affair involving lawyers and accountants. VCs take a significant stake in your company in return for their money. The earlier in the company's life they invest, the bigger the stake they take. They drive a hard bargain in the terms and conditions they apply to their investments. Dealing with professional VCs is not for the amateur or the faint-hearted. In addition, unless you have a successful track record in creating businesses or you have a truly stunning breakthrough idea that you can demonstrate through a prototype, you are unlikely to get their attention at this stage.

Thankfully you can get funding in a much more informal way through business angels. These are rich individuals who invest their own money in new businesses. Business angels are always on the lookout for great ideas and enthusiastic people to invest in.

There is much less formality with such investments and you often get a mentor as well as an investor. Some angels have even organized themselves into easy-to-access networks. Furthermore, they have good links with the big professional VC funds, can make the right introductions and are able to help you to navigate through any potential pitfalls when you need to move to Stage 3. Personally, I'm really keen on this route as a means of early funding. We used it at my new venture, Garlik, and we are in good company: the most impressive new business in the last 20 years was started with a $100,000 cheque from a business angel. The company I'm talking about is Google.

To find a business angel, just type 'business angels' into an Internet search engine. You'll be surprised how many there are. There are several websites that provide plenty of advice and actively solicit investment proposals. Three cheers again for the Internet – it's changed everything in so many ways for would-be entrepreneurs.

3. The professional VC

The majority of businesses initially funded by angels move on to professional VC funding to drive their growth. Whether and when you do this depends how much growth potential there is in your business and how much money you need. Going via the angel route first gives you a much better chance of getting a professional VC's attention and getting a good deal.

The advantages of VCs are obvious. They can provide enough investment to drive your business forward and access to professionals who know how to maximize the value of the business.

When it comes to disadvantages, there are two pitfalls to beware of. Firstly, you usually lose control of the company – this is a psychological impossibility for some entrepreneurs. It need not reduce the money you make, however; as Mo Ibrahim, founder of Celtel said: 'I'd rather have a smaller stake in a very large company than a large stake in a very small company.' He ended up owning 21% of a $3bn company and did very well indeed. The founders of the biggest VC-funded companies are among the richest people in the world: Microsoft, Apple, Google and Skype, to name but four, used VC funding at this stage of their development.

As long as you approach VCs with your eyes open, they are very powerful partners in creating a valuable business.

At this point I'd like to offer some words of wisdom from Nigel Grierson, Managing Partner of Doughty Hanson Technology Ventures, one of Europe's biggest and most successful Venture Funds. I asked Nigel what advice he would give to someone contemplating VC investment:

'We back people, first and foremost. We back people who show enthusiasm and commitment – you don't have to have a track record of creating new businesses but there must be a reason to believe you have the skills and determination to make something big happen; you can come up with solutions to the inevitable problems and twists and turns all new businesses face; and you can and will change direction when needed.

'At Intel I backed Brent Hoberman and Martha Fox with Lastminute.com. They had no real experience I could bank on and their idea wasn't that radical (an Internet travel agent), but I was almost mesmerized by their enthusiasm, passion and their no-kidding attitude.

'After people, we look for a product or technology that can establish a leadership position and for which there is a big market. We like big aggressive visions presented by people who clearly demonstrate they understand what it's going to take to make that vision real.

'We are not impressed by people who tell us all they need is 3% penetration of a large market – that's hard to achieve and harder to defend. We back things that can be market leaders.

'I like renegades and mavericks, people who can face up to and overcome fear and caution.

'I don't like dictators, people who think they are always right and don't listen. I like strong leaders and people who make firm decisions.

'I like people who understand that 20% of 100m is better than 51% of 20m, and more likely as well.'

4. The IPO or the trade sale

VCs don't hold investments for long – three to seven years would be normal. As the value of the company grows, it is quite usual for several rounds of VC funding to be raised at increasing valuations. Eventually, though, the VCs realize their investments through either an IPO (initial public offering) or a trade sale (i.e. selling your company to a bigger company).

An IPO (also called a float) means offering some of your shares – at least 20% – to public investors: insurance companies, unit trusts, pension funds and the general public, and listing the company on the stock exchange. You will know what your personal stake is worth on paper and after a while you can gradually sell shares for cash, if you wish. You regain control of the direction of the company after an IPO (although you generally only hold a minority of the shares): the public shareholders play little or no role in the management of the company, leaving that to you and the directors. They can quite easily get rid of you, though, if things aren't working out. Apple, Google and Microsoft all went through successful IPOs.

A trade sale is different. Most of them work like this:

- You get some money up front. The amount depends on the sale price, but most of it comes after a three-year period (often termed a 'work-out').
- You stay with the company during the work-out and the amount of money you get at the end of that time depends on both the initial sale price and how well the company has done since it was sold.
- After the work-out you lose management and strategic control of the company, and you probably leave.
- On some trade sales you take the money and leave immediately. Your company normally has to be fairly mature (i.e. it makes predictable profits that don't depend on you personally) for this to happen.

Some recent examples of trade sales include Skype, which was sold to eBay, and Celtel, which became the subject of a bidding war by larger companies that wanted to acquire it ahead of a planned IPO and was eventually sold to the Kuwait mobile operator MTC.

VCs like to control which route the company takes – an IPO or trade sale. It's impossible to predict in advance which route that will be because there are so many variables. However, a determined founder who remains important to the company's future performance has significant influence on the chosen route.

Variations on the growth route

There are a number of possible variations on the growth route, but the principles generally remain the same. You don't allow the growth potential of the company to be constrained by how much money you can afford to invest in it personally or by the company's own ability to generate the cash it needs to grow. Instead, you bring in external investors with the objective of owning a smaller slice of a much bigger pie.

The three variations worth considering are as follows:

1   Going direct to professional VCs at Stage 2 rather than via angel investors. If you are confident in your ability to handle the negotiations and you have a sufficiently compelling proposition to attract their attention, by all means pitch to a VC at Stage 2. If you get rejected you will at least get some valuable feedback and you can then go out and seek angel funding before returning to the VCs later.

2   As an alternative to angels at Stage 2 or VCs at Stage 3, you could seek a corporate investor. Occasionally a large company sees a strategic reason to back entrepreneurs and invest in a new venture. A well-known example of a corporate investment is Direct Line Insurance, which benefited in its early days from the Royal Bank of Scotland's investment. (RBS now owns all of it.) The best recent example is Waitrose's stake in home grocery company Ocado. This type of funding can seem like the best of both worlds: the investor's demands are softer than those from professional VCs, there is often a willingness to make larger investments than VCs will consider and they can provide a lot of operational support. The downside is that you can be vulnerable to changes in management and strategy of the investor. This sort of money is also quite hard to find. All of the investments of this type I made when I was CEO of Mercury and Egg came from personal introductions. So if you are interested in this sort of investment:

    –   tell all of your friends and contacts you are seeking an investor and ask them if they know any companies who may be interested

    –   keep your eyes open for news of big companies setting up 'innovation units' or 'business incubators' (in financial newspapers or on the Internet) and, if you find any which are relevant, approach them directly.

3   At Stage 3 you could raise further money and achieve a public listing all in one go by listing on the alternative investment market (AIM). This is like the stock market but more appropriate for small, growing companies. Your accountant and any angel investors can advise you at the right time whether this step is appropriate for you. My own view is that while valuations on AIM can be high, it's not easy for founders to realize value until the company is acquired by a larger company via a trade sale or listed on the main stock exchange via an IPO.

The bootstrap route

As a complete alternative, you could bootstrap your company over the long term. This route involves funding your business yourself, often with investments from friends and family, and maybe a small loan, until it becomes self-funding. The principle in this case is to constrain the growth of the company in order to keep 100% of it for as long as possible. This can be appropriate for Web software companies, where the initial investment is largely in time and brain power and where advertising revenues can grow quickly. However, it's a bit of a lottery as to whether you get noticed, because you don't have enough money to invest in significant promotion. It can also take a long time before the business takes off. Nevertheless, many of the big Web 2.0 successes (such as Facebook, Digg, Craigslist and Second Life) funded themselves this way.

Many of the famous individual success stories you might have read about (Alan Sugar, Felix Dennis, James Dyson and Richard Branson) also followed this route.

The big advantage of this method is that, if you are successful, by the time you come to raise external money you can do so on terms that keep majority ownership of the company in your hands. Not only does this give you a sense of complete control, but it can also make you very rich indeed.

However, you should also be aware of the disadvantages. Notably, you can end up working on a shoestring so tight that you can't afford professional help and you can't pay yourself a salary in the early days. This means potentially condemning yourself to years of financial struggle and intense hard work, seven days a week. James Dyson went right to the brink by mortgaging his home to fund his business well before he was sure it would generate the cash to pay the interest. Some entrepreneurs will tell you they put their lives on hold during this period of struggle, often putting their health and relationships at risk. Some are honest enough to admit that they only started living once they became rich.

In addition, you may end up constraining the size and growth potential of your idea, i.e. you could end up owning 100% of a small, practically worthless company. You may lose more than you can afford using this route or you may fall out with friends and family if you lose their money.

Is there such a thing as choice?

Many people think that when it comes to funding, they really don't have any choice – they will have to try and scrape together enough money to take the bootstrap route.

This is absolutely not true – not these days. If you follow my advice all the way through, you will have an idea that works, a plan that works, a real understanding of what it's going to take to pull it off and a powerful pitch to any potential investor. This will distinguish you from 90% of people who present their ideas to potential investors, and give you a real chance of following the growth route. If at first you don't succeed in finding an investor, do keep trying!

'We had real trouble funding the company. The bank wouldn't lend us any money and we were turned down by numerous VCs and angel investors. In desperation we sent an email to all of our Outlook contacts, asking if anyone knew anybody rich. We got two responses and as a result one of them, Maurice Pinto, an American, funded us with £250,000 for a 20% stake in the company. Ten per cent of the shares are in an employees' trust and the founders still own the remainder.'

Richard Reed, co-founder, Innocent Drinks

Do something

Ask yourself the following questions:

- Could you plausibly raise enough money from yourself, your friends and family to cover what you think you need to start the business and take it up to the point where it is generating reasonable amounts of revenue?
- How much vitality have you got? Can you keep going when all around you are flagging?
- Can you survive without a regular or guaranteed income from the new business for a year or two?
- Are you uncomfortable leading a company where you have to look after all the shareholders' interests?
- Do you believe that however well you do, your company will never be worth more than £20m?

If you answered 'yes' to all five questions, the bootstrap route may be the most appropriate way to fund your business. Answering 'no' to any of the questions means the growth route or one of its variations could be more appropriate.

Long shots

Before we leave the subject of funding, let's have a look at three long shots. They are worth considering briefly, even if you then immediately dismiss them.

Inventuring

Inventuring, a term coined by Buckland and Birkinshaw (2003), comes about when a new idea originates within a big company. In order to implement it they create a new business. Later the new business may be sold, floated on the stock market or reabsorbed back into the company that funded it in the first place. This was the route I took with Firstdirect and Egg. Other examples include Vodafone (which started as an idea within a company called Racal), Freeserve (which started as an idea within Dixons) and the many new companies that have been created and spun out of the Virgin Group (e.g. Virgin Atlantic).

If you are an executive in a big company with a great idea that really needs a new business and/or a new brand to bring it to life, this can be the way to go. It is particularly appropriate where you need a lot of money to build the business (beyond a $20m initial investment) and where the assets and status of the parent company are useful to you. There is more security for the founder in these situations and salaries tend to be higher. There is still potential for an IPO (such as Egg or Freeserve) or demerger (such as Vodafone), which can make it a route to significant wealth for the founders.

It sounds great and, on the whole, it is. On the downside, you have to continually fight to avoid getting caught up in the corporate fog and treacle of the parent. You should also be aware that this type of funding is extremely rare. Time and time again, people ask me how I ever managed to persuade Midland Bank to invest in Firstdirect and Prudential to invest in Egg. The answer in both cases is that:

- I knew the key decision-maker well
- the key decision-maker wanted to do something that they believed needed a more entrepreneurial approach than they would get in the parent company
- I understood how the investment made strategic sense for them
- I'm good at making truly compelling pitches.

If those four things apply to you and your idea, go for it; otherwise, don't waste your time.

Borrowing from the bank

Every bank has a network of small business advisors and special packages for start-up businesses. Look at your bank's website and you will find a lot of useful information. It's worth making an appointment with one of the small business advisors. You are going to need a business bank account at some point and maybe a facility to accept credit card payments, so you definitely need to build a relationship.

If you are looking to the bank to fund your business, however, you are likely to be disappointed. Although banks do provide funding to new businesses, they don't really have the products to fund entrepreneurial, fast-growing new businesses. Banks like businesses with tangible assets (e.g. buildings and equipment) and cash flows that are reasonably certain. If your business idea is like that, great, talk to the bank, but most won't be.

You are likely to seek funding to develop intangible assets such as software, a brand, a culture and a marketing campaign. Most entrepreneurial businesses make losses in the early years while they are building these assets. Early cash flows are usually highly unpredictable. None of this is good news for bank funding.

Government or EU grants

Both the Government and the EU have put a lot of effort into encouraging entrepreneurial start-ups. There are support networks, advice centres, grants and subsidies available in the right circumstances. Type 'enterprise grants' and 'support for new businesses' into an Internet search engine and see for yourself. You can also ask your bank for help – most of the small business advisors know their way around this area very well.

From what I have heard, you may well get some great advice and even some good-quality mentoring – but you should be prepared for a slow and somewhat bureaucratic process, and quite a lot of strings attached to any grant.

My advice would be to follow another funding route and then work with your bank and/or your accountant to determine if it is worth the effort to seek a grant or subsidy as a supplement to your main funding.

Size matters

Some founders and many investors like to get a sense of how big the company they are setting out to build could potentially be and what it could be worth to them personally. At this stage this will be very approximate indeed, particularly given the fact that the way new businesses are valued as they are growing changes constantly. But if you want to get a sense for yourself or if potential investors are asking you to estimate what sort of value you are likely to create, here are some rules of thumb:

Look at your financial plan and estimate the profits you might make in five years' time if all goes well. The potential value you can create with your initial idea will likely be somewhere between a 10 and 50 times multiple of that profit.

Factors that affect the multiple are:

- Scale – bigger businesses (above £50m profit p.a. or serving more than five million consumers) are more valuable than smaller ones.
- Scope – international businesses are more valuable than domestic ones.
- Quality of profits – businesses with profits that are based on recurring subscription revenues or on predictable advertising revenues are more valuable than those based on non-recurring product sales.
- Growth potential – businesses that have a lot of scope for further growth are more valuable than those that do not.
- Customer type – companies serving affluent consumers are more valuable than those serving less affluent consumers. Companies serving consumers tend to be more valuable than business-to-business companies.

If I'm looking for billion-dollar ideas, I'm generally looking for the potential to exceed £50m p.a. in profit and/or to serve more than five million consumers, and to have international potential.

In terms of how much money you might make personally, once more it's going to be a rough estimate at this stage. With that caveat, I'd say that if you followed the growth route, founders can expect between 10 and 40% of the value to accrue to them. Following the bootstrap route would imply 50–100% of the value to founders.

Recruiting a team

As well as funding, you also need to turn your thoughts to assembling the group of people who will join you in implementing your idea. It will be very hard if you choose to go it alone – this is actually very rare in the early days of business. It's also rare to follow any sort of formal recruitment process when you are just starting out. People tend to work with business partners they already know.

> 'It's very hard, almost impossible to do it on your own. One of my biggest priorities has always been to have a great team around me. I try to surround myself with appetite and hunger as well as loyal co-workers who can play off each others strengths.'

Robert Senior, founding partner of award-winning advertising agency, Fallon

If you are enthusiastic, committed and have been communicating widely, a bunch of potential collaborators will have probably found you by now. If not, send out requests to literally everyone you know – make the email wires buzz – and ask everyone whether they know anyone worthy who might be interested in joining you. If all else fails, type 'finding business partners' into an Internet search engine. You will find masses of websites dedicated to putting entrepreneurs in touch with potential collaborators.

Obviously, you don't need a lot of people on board right now – as few as just two of you is fine. Make sure the blend feels right, though, as you will be spending a lot of time together. Make sure your team has a stake in the company's success – that means you have to give up some ownership rights even if you take the bootstrap route.

Producing a business plan

The following steps will guide you through the process of producing a business plan that you can pitch to potential investors:

1   Go back and rewrite the final chapter of your soap opera. This will give you a new and more powerful expression of what you are setting out to create – the grand vision of a Bold and Inspiring Future that will enrol whoever is providing your funding. It will also re-engage you in the excitement of implementing your big idea and reignite your enthusiasm.

2   Come up with a theory of how you are going to beat actual and potential competitors, and a theory of how you are going to make money – many people call this a *business model*. I say 'theory', because almost everyone will tell you they ended up making money in a very different way than they had originally envisaged. You do have to start somewhere, though, and it's important you have at least some idea of where revenues will come from and when and how you are going to make a profit from them.

3   Go out and find as many critics of your idea, your funding plan and your business model as you can. Use what they have to say to sharpen everything up and help you identify the issues you are going to have to take on to make the idea successful. Produce your definitive Intelligent Insights list and the corresponding statements of intent.

4   Now you are ready to actually produce your financial plan. The most important feature of this is to specify

and justify the initial amount of investment you are seeking. It usually makes sense to raise a relatively small amount of money to start with. You only need to get hold of enough money for the first few steps. You are normally giving part of the company away in return for the cash. The value people place on your company at the beginning is usually low, so anything other than a very modest investment could mean giving up a large chunk of the company. The value of the company will grow as you progress, so you will be able to obtain more money while giving away less of the company in future funding rounds. Funding a new idea a step at a time is a good idea for everyone – it limits the loss if things go wrong. It's much easier to find funding for a sensible first step than for the whole amount of cash the business will need until it becomes self-funding. On the other hand, you don't want to be worrying about raising money just as you have launched the product, so your initial funding should take you to a point well before actual launch (e.g. to a prototype or a pilot) or up to a year beyond.

So decide which funding method you are going to go for and work out how much cash you need to get there. If you find that too difficult, then you either haven't got the idea clear enough yet, haven't done enough thinking about what it's going to take to make it happen or you haven't got the right mix of skills in your team. If any of those are a problem, go back and sort them out before you go any further.

Now go ahead and produce a first-cut financial plan with the following contents:

1 **The opportunity:** Your vision of what you are seeking to create and why.

2 **The people:** Introduce yourself and your team, your skills, and all the reasons why you can be trusted with this investment.

3 **The product:** What are you seeking to build initially?

4 **The customers:** Who needs it, how many of them are there and where are they – just in the UK or are you thinking internationally? Is it aimed at consumers or businesses, or both? (If you don't have a marketing whiz on board, you may need to get some professional help on this one or use the free marketing resources scattered across the Internet to get an approximate answer.)

5 **The operation, sales and marketing:** What's it going to take for you to take the product to market, sell it and service it? How do you propose to do that?

6 **Implementation issues:**
   – Your statements of intent, to disarm the critics.
   – How are you going to build the product and the sales and service operation?
   – What technology does it need?
   – What's novel? What problems are you going to have to solve?
   – When will you launch?
   – What are the interim milestones before launch?
   – What period would you like the initial investment to cover? (For example: the point at which you are self-funding [although it's unlikely an early stage investor would go for that one], a year beyond launch, a working prototype.)

7 **The business model:**
   - How are you thinking about generating revenues?
   - Who do you expect your main competitors to be?
   - How will you stay ahead of the competition and people who copy your idea?
   - What are your projected revenues and costs over time?
   - What overheads are projected over time?
8 **The projected financials:** Five-year profit and loss projections as you currently see them, although a sensible investor will take these with a pinch of salt and they are little more than educated guesses at this stage, and a cash flow statement covering the same period. Cash flow projections to significant milestones:
   - Launch of products to customers.
   - Launch plus a year.
   - Cash break-even.
9 **The exit route:** Investors will know more about this than you do, but it's wise to put in a couple of statements such as 'Exit could be via IPO (put in a date where your revenues are showing strong growth and you are either profitable or can confidently predict profit) or via a trade sale'.
10 **The offer of shares:** You need to specify how much of the company you are going to give investors for their money. You can make an initial stab at this (with the help of an accountant, ideally) and then get ready for a negotiation.

Be sure to put a two-page summary of the key points in the plan on the front and remember to get an accountant and a lawyer to check it and add the usual legal notices and disclaimers before you show it to anyone. Ask an accountant or lawyer about current regulations for making an offer of shares in a private company.

Making your pitch

Once you have a business plan, and if you are seeking funding from anybody other than yourself, the rest of the team or family and friends, then you are going to have to make a pitch to investors. Remember you will probably also need to have built a prototype, model or demonstration of your product idea before you pitch for external funding.

The pitch should take 20–30 minutes and should cover:

- the vision – the Bold and Inspiring Future that you are committed to and why you are committed to it
- the team – who you are and why they should back you
- your initial product(s) and the characteristics and size of the target market
- how you propose to take the product to market and sell it
- why the product will work – the unmet emotional and functional needs you are meeting with the product and for whom
- the key things you need to put in place to implement the products
- key milestones for the next two years
- the first step and how much money you need to get there
- the business model – how will you beat potential competitors and make money
- an outline of financial projections.

Do something

It's a good idea to produce and practise your pitch right now. Come up with a pitch as I've described above and practise on whatever friendly audience you can get your hands on.

Here are some tips for delivering your the pitch:

- Hold nothing back. Let your enthusiasm and commitment shine through. Leave them with one clear impression: these guys really aren't kidding about this – they mean it.

- Make sure you really demonstrate that your idea meets a clear need (current or predicted) for a defined group of customers (business or consumer).

- Make sure you really demonstrate that you understand what issues you are going to have to address to make this happen.

- Tell them clearly why they should trust you to pull it off and show them any evidence you have that supports this.

- Don't use bullet points on PowerPoint slides as your script – use slides to illuminate what you are saying, not to repeat it.

- Sum it all up in a powerful one-minute pitch.

If you have done everything I've suggested so far, you are in really great shape. Remember the power of bold commitment – let nothing stop you now.

6

Know your ends from your means

'However beautiful the strategy, you should occasionally look at the results.'

Winston Churchill

By now, you could have a credible financial plan, an assembled team and investors that you have convinced to back you. At least a few people will have believed in you enough to join your team and at least one person will have had enough faith to write you a cheque. You should take time to appreciate those things as genuine accomplishments – few people have the courage to take an idea this far.

You will have come a long way, but the hard work is really just beginning. When you have raised enough money to fund your idea, it's time to focus on putting together a plan of action to get the show on the road.

Most of the work you have done so far is to define the following:

- What your idea is.
- What you are seeking to accomplish in total with this idea and what's important about how you go about it (the Bold and Inspiring Future you created for yourselves and others when you wrote the final chapter of your soap opera).
- What products and services you are creating for whom.
- What financial results you are seeking to achieve.
- What major issues are involved in getting this done.

There has been a limited description of 'the means' (i.e. how you intend to achieve your goals) in the business plan. However, so far you have only done enough to convince yourselves and your investors that you know what needs to be taken on.

In putting together a plan of action to finally get the show on the road we will be moving away from the what (the ends) and focusing on the how (the means).

You've got to have a plan

How you approach a task is usually referred to as 'a strategy'. The strategy is always the means to an end; it is a plan for achieving medium- and long-term objectives.

Business strategy is an important topic for companies. It is especially important for large companies whose business is predictable enough to plan over the medium and long term. Much of this planning attempts to anticipate and prepare for any new competitors they are likely to face in the future, and to prepare for emerging technologies that will be useful to them. Fast-growing start-up businesses are often more concerned with creating the future than anticipating it – this is the main reason why successful entrepreneurs can be so dismissive of strategy. Many of them will say that 'strategy is the story you tell about how you got somewhere after you got there'.

In many ways, that's true. It's ludicrous to think you can produce a plan for the early years of a fast-growing entrepreneurial business that remains relevant over more than about 12 months. Indeed, it is central to my own philosophy that you shouldn't over-plan: you first set the goals you are committed to (the ends), working out how you get there (the means) as you go along. That's why I believe in writing the final chapter of your soap opera first.

But that final chapter is set too far out into the future to help you decide what activities you are going to focus on in first 12 months of your new business. You have to approach that ultimate goal one step at a time. In order to do this you need to set an interim goal – the ends that you are seeking to achieve in the first 12 months of the business. Then you can devise a plan to get there – the means.

This sounds easy enough, but bear in mind that things rarely go to plan. So then what do you do?

During the year you will need to change the means, taking advantage of everything you learn about what's working and what's not working. However, it is critical that you leave the ends alone. Try to keep going right to the end of the year, getting as close as you can to the interim goal you have set yourself.

At the end of the year, assess what you actually achieved and what you learnt and then decide on your next step. Create a new interim goal (the ends to which you are committed for the next 12 months) and devise a new plan to get there (the means).

This approach to planning balances focus and flexibility. There is always one source of enduring focus: your ultimate goal, the final end to which you are committed, the Bold and Inspiring Future you created in the final chapter of your soap opera. That's always your guiding star.

You have total flexibility in how you approach that ultimate goal. You always approach it a step at a time. Each year, take stock of where you are and decide what the next step is going to be. During the year, the ends you set yourself become a stop-over *en route* to your final goal. You stay focused by keep-ing those ends constant. You achieve flexibility by altering the means wherever necessary as you go along.

> '*I intuitively based many of my business strategies on the fun-damental principles of tai chi. It taught me a lot about balance, the importance of being able to adapt to forces around you and see change or competition as positive. If you have a fixed route, you're not taking into account your external environment and responding to it effectively. You need to strike the balance between being fixed and flexible. It's not always easy but it's extremely important. Lost Wax has existed since 1996 despite many difficulties and market downturns because we evolved and stayed flexible throughout hard times with our eyes on a fundamental fixed goal.*'

Tom Ilube, founder of software company Lost Wax and co-founder of Garlik

I call this approach *dynamic action planning*. I have found it in-credibly useful in staying on track towards my ultimate goal, whatever circumstances or difficulties I meet along the way. However far I've been blown off course, I always know that the next step I take will always be towards a fixed goal – and that's powerfully reassuring.

Successful entrepreneurs are instinctively flexible and ex-perimental about the means they use to achieve what they care about – the ends. In the middle of whatever chaos they are cop-ing with, they never lose sight of the ends themselves.

'It's crazy to think you can come up with a fixed strategy for a new company. You have to be flexible and re-orientate yourself as you go along.

'We plan on four levels:

1   One thing remains constant: we are always committed to creating a natural and ethical food brand, and a company which combines value and profit growth with the creation of a positive environmental and social legacy, and we want to be the best in the world at that.

2   Our interim objectives – these change as we achieve each step:
    - We started with an ambition to be London's favourite little smoothie company.
    - We moved on to an ambition to be England's and then the UK's favourite little smoothie company.
    - Our ambition now is to be Europe's favourite little smoothie company by 2010 and by 2030 the Earth's favourite little food company.

3   Our three-year strategy is aimed at taking us towards our interim objective. We review and amend this strategy every year.

4   The final level is our execution plan, which is based on one-year objectives and five key themes for the company, which are cascaded down so they become five key themes for each team and then each individual.'

Richard Reed, co-founder, Innocent Drinks

When in a hole, stop digging

The first reason to adopt this dynamic action planning approach is to prevent a common mistake that I've seen many times: people continuing to do the things they have always done, things that were successful in the past, but which will not make them successful in the future. They make an inadequate response to changing circumstances because they are not continually reassessing the means they need to adopt to get to their goal (their ends).

The most striking example for me occurred in a dinner I had with senior executives at Mercury Communications when I first arrived there as CEO in 1991.

As they spoke, I could clearly see the ambition: they had got to £1bn in revenues faster than any other company in Europe ever had before, with the intention of doubling that over the next few years. But when I asked them about their strategies and how they intended to achieve this, I got the stock response:

'Strategy's what you use to explain how you got to where you are after you've got there.'

'How did you get here?' I asked them.

'Building a competitive network to BT and using new technology so we were better and cheaper. We met so many unexpected problems along the way we couldn't possibly have planned it all in advance – we had to improvise,' was their reply.

'So of course that was successful then, but can we double revenues with the same approach – the same products as BT, but better and cheaper?' I asked.

'Er, not exactly,' they stuttered. 'There is still a lot of mileage in it, but we've taken the low-hanging fruit. BT has sorted itself out and has the same technology as us now – they can make their scale advantages count and other new competition is arriving too. Our margins are squeezed by the way price regulation works and our systems are creaking a bit: they weren't designed for a company as large as ours. And don't forget intelligent networks, multimedia, broadband, high-speed data and the emerging digital world – plenty of threats and opportunities there.'

'So what's our strategy?' I asked.

'We are reengineering all of our processes to get ahead or maybe keep up with BT on quality. We are also replacing all of our systems so they are more efficient and we have a small team looking at emerging technologies.'

'People tell me those programmes aren't really working,' I said, 'but even if it does all work, it sounds an inadequate response to the new circumstances you have described.'

One of the executives responded: 'What do you expect us to do? All of our resources and assets are focused on doing what we have always done. We can still make money that way and as for the future, everything is going to come at us in a way we can't possibly predict – we are just going to have to deal with it as it comes.'

Of course he was right. The circumstances were unpredictable and there was no way one could produce a strategic plan in advance that gave predictable results. On the other hand, their bold vision of doubling their turnover was just hot air without some planning designed to take them towards it.

The bold improvisation that had served them well to date would be needed again, but it wouldn't be enough. They needed a dynamic approach to planning that would help them amend their current approach and take some first steps towards their longer-term goal.

Where do we go from here?

The second reason to adopt a dynamic planning approach is that it allows you to invent the means as you go along without losing sight of the ends. There are many examples of successful companies that started out with big ambitions without knowing how to get there:

- The founders of Google couldn't predict what would happen when they unleashed their new search engine on the world; they didn't even have a way of generating revenues initially. Google ads, the key revenue-generating tool, was invented much later because at some point it became an important next step (means) towards their ultimate goal (end) of digitizing the world – later refined to organizing the world's information.
- Microsoft went through numerous twists and turns in fulfilling its vision of a PC on every desk and in every home. One of the key enablers of this, the Internet, only emerged as a consumer tool in the mid-1990s. Microsoft initially underestimated the importance of the Internet and other companies such as Sun and Cisco who had seen its power early seemed likely to threaten Microsoft's position as industry leaders. Microsoft grasped the Internet just in time and, with bold improvisation, reoriented the entire company and its set of products around the Internet as a means to maintain its leadership and achieve its ends.
- The mobile phone company Celtel started life as a software company before its team saw an opportunity to use its own software to bid for and win a licence to build a mobile network in Africa. Celtel seized that opportunity and used it and similar opportunities as the means that ultimately achieved founder Mo Ibrahim's end goal of a $1bn company. He was confidently expressing this goal when the software company was generating a mere $24m a year in revenue and growing only slowly.

These companies took on huge and complex challenges that caused them to change direction many times, continually reinventing themselves, their products and their services – continually reinventing their means. They improvised boldly again and again without losing sight of why they were created in the first place, their purpose, or the Bold and Inspiring Future that they were committed to – their ends.

Let's take a look at Virgin Atlantic. I know something of this story from the inside. When I was CEO at Mercury (fighting BT), we used to get together with Virgin executives (fighting BA) from time to time to compare notes. Both of us were small start-ups, fighting a giant, well-funded, former state monopoly. There was a critical difference, however – which, although painful at the time, ended up working to Virgin's advantage. BT was an ethical competitor; BA were not.

Richard Branson appeared in a TV advert endorsing Mercury after he had won a high-profile court case against BA. It was just after a newspaper headline screamed: 'Virgin screws BA.' The Mercury ad got a lot of attention and was more than worth the effort it took me to smooth ruffled feathers in BA (at that time Mercury's biggest customer).

Virgin Atlantic is an inspirational story for any budding entre-preneur. Richard Branson's ambition for Virgin Atlantic was to build a high-quality, value for money airline that would revolutionize aviation by concentrating on the customer experience rather than the logistics and the engineering. That ambition was the constant guiding star (the end to which he was committed) throughout the trials, tribulations, improvisation, innovation and courage that have today created an airline that in my opinion stands head, shoulders and entire upper torso above any other in the world.

It started in 1984 with a single leased Boeing 747-200, running a single route from Gatwick to Newark (New York's junior international airport). As a first step in a revolution, no one was taking it seriously at that point.

Richard said: 'Not one person thought it would last for more than a year.'

Indeed, a magazine survey in 1984 revealed only 10% of people would be happy to fly with Virgin. Richard wrote to the editor, thanking him for the research, and stated that they only had one plane so they could only handle 400 people a day anyway. The potential market they stated was many times their capacity.

In 1984, Virgin had no idea of the path they would ultimately take to create the award-winning airline of today, which has 38 planes (with 27 more on order) and an extensive worldwide network.

The unpredictable (and unplannable in advance) means to success included:

- Scrambling to get everything together in the early days:

'We rented a warehouse near Gatwick where we housed engineering staff and started recruiting pilots and cabin staff. We rented office space in an Air Florida Office just off Oxford Street and piggy-backed on their computer reservations system. The timetable was virtually impossible. One minute we were designing uniforms or menus, the next negotiating the aircraft lease.'
Richard Branson, 1998

- Being the first airline to offer individual TVs to their business class passengers.
- Starting flights from Heathrow in 1991, a move that provoked a violent competitive reaction from BA.

'Despite the excitement of starting our Heathrow operation in July 1991 it was clear we would not be able to expand any further for a while. In any event we couldn't offer another route for another three years until we started flying to Hong Kong in 1994. This was due to one of the fiercest and most focused and most vicious attacks ever launched by an airline against a smaller competitor.'
Richard Branson, 1998

- This apparent major setback proved, in retrospect, to be the turning point for Virgin Atlantic. BA eventually settled an action out of court in 1993 when lawyers unearthed evidence of the extraordinary lengths to which the company went to try to destroy Virgin.
- Buying new planes, expanding the route network and generally breaking new ground in passenger service, both on the ground and in the air in the 1990s.
- Introducing the first super economy service that went on to become the award-winning Premium Economy.
- Selling a 49% stake in the company to Singapore Airlines in 1999, valuing the business at a minimum of £1.225bn.
- The launch of the Upper Class Suite in 2002, which gave premium passengers the longest flat bed in the industry and a great night's sleep.

Do something

Think of something you have achieved in your personal or business life. It should be something that was difficult to accomplish, took a reasonable amount of time and effort, and required a lot of planning. Write it up as a case study similar to the Virgin Atlantic example above. Note the major milestones, the major turning points, the moments of good fortune and the times when everything seemed to be going wrong. Also note the key decisions you took along the way, the times when you had to try different approaches and the times when you had to improvise, maybe, to reach your goal.

When I ask people to do this exercise in workshops, the increase in confidence and self-belief is palpable. When you are taking on a significant new challenge, it's good to remind yourself of what you have achieved in the past.

People who make big ideas happen are able to improvise boldly without losing sight of what they were seeking to achieve in the first place. Things rarely go to plan in business so if you want to join them and live out your dream, prepare to improvise and think on your feet.

By now you should realize that this requires you to separate the ends and means. So when you make the inevitable changes of direction you are only changing the means and not becoming directionless by losing sight of the ends. You will also need to learn from everything you have tried; from what worked and what didn't, from what other companies are doing and the results they are getting. Apply this knowledge when you amend your means.

The dynamic planning approach

The most fundamental lessons I have learnt over the past 20 years about business planning are as follows:

- Your means towards your desired end are inevitably built on beliefs and assumptions because you can never entirely predict the future. So don't get upset if and when your results aren't what you were expecting, or something you didn't anticipate happens. That's just life – learn from it and move on.
- The beliefs and assumptions that drive your choice of means can become sources of rigidity. Unless challenged and re-examined on a regular basis, they can point you in the wrong direction.
- You need to see the results you are getting (good or bad) as valuable feedback about what to do next.

From these lessons I have devised a dynamic approach to planning. It gives you a practical tool to accomplish what successful entrepreneurs often do instinctively. It allows you to do the following:

> - To separate your ends and means.
> - To allow improvisation on the means without losing sight of the ultimate goal (the ends).
> - To learn what needs to be changed about the means by looking at the results you are getting and what's happening in the wider market.

Changing perspective

We tend to categorize our results as either good or bad. If they are bad, we often blame someone or something for implementing our intentions in the wrong way.

I've learned to think about results in a different way. I think results are likely to reflect the quality of the beliefs and assumptions that were behind the plan put together in the first place. At the very least I want to examine the quality of these beliefs and assumptions in the light of unexpected results.

When I say 'quality of beliefs and assumptions', I mean the level of insight contained within them and their appropriateness for the circumstances facing us now or in the future. New circumstances might mean old assumptions and beliefs that served us well in the past are no longer appropriate. In order for this feedback loop (from actual results back to assumptions and beliefs in our strategy) to work effectively, you need to rigorously separate ends from means.

The fundamental end of your strategy is the Bold and Inspiring Future you have set out to create. That is not based on beliefs and assumptions; it is simply something you have chosen to create, irrelevant of possibility. Don't allow your results to challenge that: stay committed to that end while allowing results to challenge the means you are adopting to get there.

So that's the principle: you hold the ends steady while you flex everything else. Everything you do is your means to an end. The means you come up with are always based on a set of beliefs and assumptions. Let your results challenge and amend those beliefs and assumptions – don't be precious about them. Learn as you go, a step at a time, towards your ultimate destination.

Holding a few things steady (the ends) while flexing everything else (the means) is a powerful approach. As I've suggested, it makes sense to set interim goals on the way to your ultimate goal. Let's look at a perfect example of keeping a single end fixed while being very flexible about the means of getting there.

Apollo 13

In 1996, I saw the film *Apollo 13*. This was a dramatization of the real Apollo 13 mission, the third manned lunar-landing. The spacecraft was all but destroyed by an explosion but the crew were able to use the lunar module as a lifeboat to return to Earth. I was inspired. I thought it was the best film about leadership ever made. In fact, after watching the film, I avidly read everything I could find about the real thing. So when the *Financial Times* interviewed me in 1998 as part of a series on leadership, I surprised them by saying that Gene Kranz, former Flight Director of NASA and the real hero of the Apollo 13 story, was the leader who had most inspired me.

I explained the Apollo 13 connection and the story as I'd understood it from the books.

The ground staff had to come up with a way for the crew to successfully improvise a re-entry using the scarce resources that were available on the damaged space craft and lunar module.

'"This crew is coming home. I don't give a damn about the odds, and I don't give a damn that we've never done anything like this before, flight control will never lose an American – not on my watch ..." Kranz assured them.'

Gene Kranz, 2000

He had no evidence to show that it was possible; indeed the evidence suggested otherwise. But the clear end to which he was committed was to bring his crew back alive. He made it clear to his team that their job was not to argue about whether this was possible but to get on with inventing the means:

'"Okay team, we have a hell of a problem – it is our job to figure out how to get them home," he told them. "The odds are damned long, but we are going to do it. We will develop a strategy that uses the spacecraft resources, will build and control the budgets of the electrical water life support and any other resources together. I've asked John to control that, so whatever he says goes."'

Gene Kranz, 2000

His enthusiasm infected everybody with the belief that it was possible. He gave the ground crew some rules about the means but he appealed to their creativity to invent a plan.

Eventually they were left with one problem. The crew had taken refuge in the lunar module, which had not been designed to be occupied by three people for an extended time. The air scrubbers that kept the atmosphere free of poisonous carbon dioxide had run out. The crew would die from the gases produced by their own breathing. Kranz put a team on the problem.

'"This is all they have," he said, throwing a few pieces of what looked like rubbish onto the table. "Make me a scrubber; no one leaves until I have one."

Gene Kranz, 2000

The design for an air scrubber was improvised with just seconds to spare. Exact instructions were sent to the crew and they made one from a few pieces of cardboard, a sock, a hose from a pressure suit, a plastic bag and some duct tape. Amazingly, the crew survived.

Apollo 13 can teach us some valuable lessons about getting results and making the impossible happen. Kranz was as precise about rules that applied to the means as he was about the ends. He was precise about constraints, the timescale, what was fixed and what was flexible, and the assumptions he was making (e.g. resources such as power and water). All of these things are key characteristics of a successful practical approach to producing and using a dynamic action plan.

Practical dynamic planning for new businesses

The point about dynamic planning is that it's suitable for the leadership team of new businesses (or anyone trying to implement a big idea) to use simply and cheaply. However, it's not suitable as a strategic planning tool for a major corporation, which needs a good deal more sophistication and resource. Having said that, the principles within this tool are similar to best practice planning techniques in large corporations:

> I explained my dynamic planning approach to Peter Darbee, Chairman of Pacific Gas and Electric. I added that it's probably not appropriate for large companies such as PG&E.
>
> His response was: 'Maybe not – but the principles we used were actually identical to yours. We set long-term inspirational goals which don't change and we approach them in a series of interim steps. We produce a five-year strategy, a three-year operational plan and a one-year action plan. We like to hit the goals we have set ourselves in that one-year plan, but we may have to change direction a few times to get there. Of course we thoroughly review our strategy at least once every year and of course it changes in response to new circumstances and new insights.'

I've used the tool I'm about to describe at Garlik extensively over the past two years and it has worked well. I used it successfully at Egg when, as Vice Chairman, I was leading a team building prototypes of new ideas in Internet banking.

As you definitely know by now, dynamic planning starts with a separation of ends and means. We always start with the end game: what you specified in the final chapter of your soap opera. You may have set the final scene in three or five years' time, or further into your future, but it is a true end to the story that you are currently beginning. The story is in essence an account of the journey you are embarking on, a journey with one end in mind – to make what you said in the final chapter come true.

Everything else in the journey is a means to that end. Like any journey, although there are some rules you have to follow, there are also choices to make along the way, unpredictable circumstances to face and competitive actions to respond to. Your soap opera is the story of how you undertake that journey, the milestones you set for yourself and the choices you take along the way.

So let's return to the final chapter of your soap opera. When complete, it should read something like the final chapter I produced in 1997, which ended like this:

'So that's my story. In 1998 Prudential invested in a new revolutionary financial services company that was intensely customer-focused and used emerging technology such as the Internet and digital TV. When this company launched, at least ten million customers in the UK agreed that digital banking was relevant to them. It was a company where creativity and diversity were valued and employees were free to express themselves fully. I built the business as Chief Executive and in 2000 it was floated on the Stock Exchange at a value of more than £1bn. I subsequently retired as Chief Executive and became Chairman.'

Producing the initial plan

The initial dynamic plan should cover what I call an *interim end* – it is what you seek to accomplish in the first 12 months of your business, which will be the first step towards your ultimate end. (As I said before, 12 months is a good point to set the first interim end.)

Your plan will separate this interim end year from the means of achieving it, while also being explicit about the rules and assumptions you are applying to the means. This is the key to keeping the plan dynamic enough to respond to results and changing circumstances.

The plan should be put together in a one- or two-day session with the leadership team. Remember you already have the following:

- the idea
- what you are seeking to accomplish in total with this idea (the final chapter of your soap opera)
- what products and services you are creating for whom
- what financial results you are seeking to achieve
- the big issues you need to address in achieving this.

So assemble these and your leadership team and engage in the following question:

> What are we seeking to accomplish in the next 12 months that will take us towards our ultimate goal?
>
> The answer needs to be just one or two sentences. It is an end you are creating as an interim step towards your ultimate goal.

For Egg we came up with:

> We will launch with no compromise to our principles of individualized products and customer service, and the phones will ring off the hook.

And for Garlik we came up with:

> In the next 12 months we will achieve a transformation in the company's standing amongst stakeholders by creating Garlik as a strong brand with demonstrable consumer and media appeal. We will move from an interesting opportunity to a full-on commitment amongst shareholders, employees and partners.

The characteristics of this interim goal are similar to those of the ultimate goal. The description of this interim goal needs to be:

- a desired end state, not a strategy to get there
- not financially based
- stretching but not impossible
- clear, self-explanatory, bold and exciting to you and your collaborators.

The next question to answer is the following: 'What key conditions must be satisfied in order to meet our interim goal?'

Now you are beginning to build a path towards your goal by focusing attention, effort and resources on those things that will make a real difference. However, since these are now your means to an end, you need to specify them with some ambiguity. This gives you great flexibility in how they are achieved, but just enough rigour for you to be clear on the constraints you have to work under.

For example, at Garlik we came up with:

- Launch a pilot in April 2006 to coincide with the launch of the company at the World Wide Web conference.
- Launch a live product before the end of 2006 that demonstrates the power of our technology and is a reflection of the brand purpose (giving individuals and their families real power in the use of their personal information in the digital world).
- Achieve at least 10,000 customers, and demonstrate clear revenue potential and an understanding of what it will take to sell our products.
- Achieve good press presence and favourable coverage in order to establish the Garlik brand, reputation and its values in the public's mind.

- Achieve demonstrable executive commitment and develop the Garlik culture so we can deliver the brand promise.
- Use no more than £2m of cash and be in a great position to demonstrate the financial viability of the business so that the next funding round can be achieved.

I'll just make some points about these conditions:

- Where possible, we added quantifiable measures so we could be certain about whether they had been achieved or not.
- Note the focus on cash and demonstrating the viability of the business to actual and potential investors – always a key issue for new businesses. You may well change the business model a few times in the early days, but it's vital you keep demonstrating that you have a theory of value-generation and some evidence that there is a viable business model of some sort. If you are bootstrapping, you are going to have to worry mostly about generating enough cash to keep going.
- Note the focus on establishing the company's brand and culture; these are how you implement what is important to you about the manner in which you go about things. For example, the Egg brand was strong on individualized solutions and the Egg culture was strong on allowing people to be themselves – both reflecting our commitment to respect and empower individual differences and individual preferences as we implemented the idea that became Egg.

- Note the use of pilots in Garlik. In many circumstances, prototypes and pilots are really useful tools to get things right before you spend big development money.

Your next question is: 'Who is going to be accountable for the delivery of each condition?' Assign just one person to each condition or you will fail. One person can have more than one condition, though:

- Make sure the whole team is prepared to support each accountable person in his or her role.
- Give the person concerned the opportunity to make requests of the rest of the team for support or assistance.
- The method in which the accountable person goes about achieving their results is commonly referred to as tactics, and you leave that up to them within the bounds of agreements on resources and values.
- Don't let this accountability conversation close too soon – you may need to come back to it again and again over several days. It only ends well when:
  - the team is clear they can rely on each accountable person to deliver with the resources and budget they have been allocated (which will be less than they have asked for)
  - each accountable person is clear what they have taken on, is committed to it full-on, is clear what the resources and constraints are and is clear they are supported by the rest of the team.

Write your plan on a single sheet of A4 and give everyone a copy. Pin some up on the walls as well. I've given an example of such a plan in Table 6.1 – you can use the same sort of layout for yours.

Table 6.1 Garlik initial plan, 2006

Company purpose: the end to which we are committed	To give individuals and their families real power in the use of their personal information in the digital world.
Interim end for 2006	By the end of the year, we will have achieved a transformation in the company's standing among stakeholders by creating Garlik as a strong brand with demonstrable consumer/media appeal. We move from being a semi-committed exciting, speculative adventure to a full-on commitment.
Conditions of satisfaction and accountabilities (Accountable person to produce measures for the satisfactory achievement of each condition)	Launch a pilot in April 2006 to coincide with the launch of the company at the World Wide Web conference (Tom). Launch a live product before the end of 2006 that demonstrates the power of our technology and is a reflection of the brand purpose (giving individuals and their families real power in the use of their personal information in the digital world) (Charles). Achieve at least 10,000 customers, and demonstrate clear revenue potential and an understanding of what it will take to sell our products (Cottie). Achieve good press presence and favourable coverage in order to establish the Garlik brand, reputation and its values in the public's mind (Cottie). Achieve demonstrable executive commitment and develop the Garlik culture so we can deliver the brand promise (Mike). Use no more than £2m of cash and be in a great position to demonstrate the financial viability of the business so that the next funding round can be achieved (Tom).

I'll cover how you use this plan of action in Chapter 9, but for now, I'll just note that you should reassess it at least every three months or whenever something unexpected happens (good or bad). Take a good, hard look at your results and what they tell you about the beliefs and assumptions that are behind your means, and be prepared to flex and improvise. Never mess with the ends!

Start this whole process again 10–12 months on so that you enter the second year of your business well-prepared, with a new plan of action. Building on what you have achieved and learned so far, produce a plan for the next 12 months that takes you ever closer to your ultimate goal.

Do something

Produce a draft dynamic action plan for the first 12 months of your business.

You can do this alone but if you have one or more people already working with you or interested in joining, involve them as well. Go through the process of creating the plan exactly as I have described in this chapter.

When it comes to assigning accountabilities, just write down the sort of person you will need to be accountable for a particular condition.

When you are starting a business for real you need to do this planning exercise rigorously and with your whole team, as I described earlier in the chapter.

7

Brand and reputation matters

'It takes 20 years to build a reputation and five minutes to ruin it. If you think about that, you'll do things differently.'

Warren Buffett

So far, even if all you've done is contemplate taking the next step towards your Bold and Inspiring Future, you've already been on quite a journey. Imagine if you had taken the plunge and produced a business plan, an action plan and found funding. Perhaps you have? Either way, you should feel good about gearing yourself towards lighting up the world around you with your big idea.

If and when you get to the point of launching, that's exactly what you'll have to do: light up the world so that it knows your big idea exists. This takes us into the territory of brand and reputation, and the key tools you can use to tell the world you exist – marketing, publicity and advertising.

Painting a clear picture of the sort of brand you want to create is a fundamental first step to creating any new business. Many people think of a brand as just a name. While this is an important feature, it's by no means the heart of the matter. At its most powerful, a brand represents your promise of how you run your business and what customers (and employees) can expect from you.

In the entrance to the offices of leading brand consultancy Identica – we used them to help design the Garlik brand – is a large plaque. It reads:

> 'A brand is a promise; a strong brand is a promise which is kept.'

And that's about as good a definition as you are likely to find.

A brand can do three things for you:

1   Create economic value – a powerful brand generates value, either in the ability to charge a premium or in reducing the costs of getting new customers.
2   Act as a competitive shield – making it much harder for other companies to take the space you have laid claim to; even if they have a superior product, they have to create a reputation that surpasses yours.
3   Act as internal glue – a brand can and should be the centrepiece of a powerful culture.

Strange but true

To begin to get a sense of the power of a well-established brand, consider the following facts.

Intelligent ATMs?

In 1990, Midland Bank and Firstdirect ran identical satisfaction surveys among their respective customers. One of the questions concerned satisfaction with the Midland ATM network, which actually provided services to both sets of customers. Ninety per cent of the Firstdirect customers were very satisfied, compared with less than 50% of Midland's customers. Yet when you asked questions about service expectations, Firstdirect customers were much more demanding. Were the ATMs intelligent enough to recognize a Firstdirect customer and provide a better service – or could there be another explanation?

Still cheaper after all these years?

In 1994, a survey among potential and actual Mercury customers (business and consumer) revealed the perception that Mercury provided much better value than BT. Satisfaction levels with the quality of service were identical, but Mercury was perceived as having a much lower prices. This had been true three years before, but it wasn't in 1994: the gap in prices had narrowed considerably. Indeed, some of our prices were nearly the same as BT's. Our advertising focused on our ease of use, not our prices. So why were we still perceived as being considerably cheaper?

All publicity is good publicity

In 1998, soon after the launch of Egg, I was interviewed on a BBC consumer complaints show. They had received a number of complaints about how long it was taking for Egg to open savings accounts after receiving a cheque in the post and how long it took to get through on the phone. It had all been true – we had been absolutely swamped, but by the time the programme aired we had ironed out all the kinks and things were running reasonably smoothly again. The programme put together a very sarcastic film to introduce the interview, using every Egg pun you can imagine. As the film faded out, the presenter started to rip me apart. But despite this public humiliation, that evening we had more than double the usual number of phone calls from people wanting to open an account. What caused this strange reaction?

Deflowered Virgin

Sometime in the 1990s, I was travelling from London to Birmingham in the first-class compartment of a Virgin train. The train stopped in the middle of nowhere for an hour. A member of staff appeared at last, wearing the distinctive Virgin uniform.

'There's a train broken down in front of us,' he said. 'We are going to have to push it out of the way.' A lady in her 70s, who had been entertaining me with tales of her youth during the delay, misunderstood and got on her high horse magnificently. 'If you think I'm getting out of the carriage, getting down on that track and pushing anything, you have another thing coming,' she said defiantly.

The guy from Virgin walked away without a word, leaving me to explain our train would do the pushing, not the passengers. But the point of this story is that I was so stunned when he first appeared that I was barely listening to what he had to say. He looked sloppy and unkempt. His uniform was dirty and ill-fitting. Why was I so shocked at that?

Reputation matters

At the heart of all these questions is one central truth: never underestimate the importance of your reputation.

A company's reputation has economic value:

- Egg's reputation in 2003 as both the leader in Internet banking and a cool consumer champion meant that it could get new customers at less than half the cost of the competition.
- Virgin Atlantic can charge a considerable premium on its price compared to BA based on its reputation.

Your company's reputation can also act as a competitive shield:

- Mercury's reputation for being better value than BT still affected buying decisions long after prices evened out.
- One executive I know told me that he always bought on-line from John Lewis. 'Ah, never knowingly undersold,' I said. 'No,' he replied. 'Even if they were more expensive, I would value the fact that if anything goes wrong – and it often does buying online – they will take care of it without fuss.' When I asked him to give me an example, he didn't have one – it was the reputation that counted.
- Firstdirect's reputation for stellar service made it hard for others to compete with them on that basis alone.

Brand and culture

A brand can be the centrepiece of a powerful culture. In fact, that's what it should be. A brand represents a promise to employees as much as to customers and creating a culture is the way you deliver both of those promises.

Rupert Howell was a founding partner of the advertising agency Howell Henry Chaldecott Lury (HHCL). HHCL was behind the campaigns that launched Firstdirect and Egg. It was also at the heart of the Mercury consumer story – from nothing to a £1bn-plus brand. HHCL was named one of the five great agencies of all time in 2006. When Rupert speaks about reputation, branding and marketing, he has earned the right to have the world listen. Here is the invaluable advice he gave me:

'Brands should be created from the inside out. A strong brand is an authentic expression of what the founders really believe and reflects the culture they are going to build. You start with that

premise, then you use consumer research to get the products right. You don't start with consumer research and decide where to position your brand so consumers will like and support you. That's spin and it gets everyone a bad name. A brand needs to live up to its promises.'

Two of the most successful advertising campaigns of recent times were Ronseal ('It does exactly what it says on the tin') and the AA ('To our members we're the fourth emergency service'). Fundamentally, both Ronseal and the AA were communicating with great authenticity. Their campaigns simply articulated what people already knew was true in a way that resonated well with their employees and their actual and potential customers. People agreed with their statements and therefore regarded them as honest, reliable brands.

'We knew we had serious work to do when we were asked to reposition the Skoda brand in 2000. It was a renowned brand for all the wrong reasons. Six out of ten people said they wouldn't buy a Skoda. Children would cry in the showrooms because they didn't want to be dropped off at school in one.

'In this case we had to embrace the negative and be brutally honest about the fact people thought they were rubbish. Indeed, Skoda was a zeitgeist for emerging honesty amongst brands and customers responded well to that. We knew it was bad, and so did the customer and we played off that knowledge. Brutal honesty led to a definite shift – it's now the fastest selling car in Europe but it's a shame things got so critical before it was remedied. Now only one-third of people would never buy a Skoda – that's not bad.'

Robert Senior, founding partner of UK agency of the year, Fallon

'I believe a brand should reflect what you believe in – that's what we set out to create at Innocent. The culture is totally aligned with the brand. Our brand values are reflected in our slogan 'little tasty drinks and nothing but fruit' and in our humour – the little jokes on the bottles. We call them innocent because our drinks are always completely pure, fresh and unadulterated. Anything you ever find in an Innocent bottle will always be 100% natural and delicious.'

Richard Reed, co-founder, Innocent Drinks

That's about as pure as it can get. For most brands it's more complicated than that, but the key thought remains: the brand must deliver what it promises; the brand experience as a whole must match up to what it claims to deliver.

I tried to communicate authentically when I was interviewed about Egg's shortcomings. I admitted that we had made lots of mistakes and that we felt really bad about letting customers down. I also admitted that we had a way to go before we arrived where we wanted to be. As I left, someone said to me 'That was unusually honest' – it seemed to pay off.

The Virgin brand screams consumer champion at me each time I see it. All of my experiences of Virgin lead to expect a service that demonstrates that they have understood what really matters to their customers, along with a sense of fun.

'Virgin works hard at developing its image from its distinctive, uplifting logo to the way in which the businesses are presented.'

Richard Branson, 1998

This explains why I was so shocked at my experience on the Virgin train – it was a horrible mismatch of expectation and reality.

'In some ways we have been the victims of our own success in that train passengers expected that as soon as Virgin had taken over a miraculous change would take place.'

Richard Branson, 1998

Richard's right – it is a little unfair, but what a demonstration of the power of a brand.

We launched Firstdirect on a Sunday. We took calls immediately and started opening accounts right away on the phone. It was previously unthinkable to launch a new service on a Sunday, let alone a bank, but it was the best way we could think of to demonstrate we were exactly what it said on the tin: a bank that was open 24 hours a day, seven days a week.

Reputation can be lost in an instant

This is a fundamental lesson. Perception affects – some would say creates – reality. If you continue to do a good job and communicate authentically, people tend to relate to you based on your reputation. They experience what they are expecting, unless something jolts them out of that mindset – that's when you can be ruined in an instant.

Remember Teflon Tony Blair? He swam smoothly through numerous difficulties based on his reputation as 'a pretty straight sort of a guy'. Once that reputation was fatally damaged by the furore about weapons of mass destruction and the Iraq war, he could do no right. An apparently impregnable hero had suddenly descended all the way to zero.

It's the same in the corporate world. I remember being surprised by the way banking analysts used to idolize Northern Rock. There were occasional grumbles in the consumer finance press about its approach, and neither its pricing, marketing nor business model appealed to me. But Northern Rock had a stellar reputation in the City for years. That reputation was savaged beyond repair in just one weekend by the queues of people outside the branches desperately trying to get their money.

Believe me – however small you are when you start out, it's worth taking care to create the reputation and brand you want and making sure you protect it.

Do something

Make a list of three to five of your favourite brands and write down for each brand:

- The first thought that goes through your mind when you start to think about the brand and bring the image of the logo into your consciousness.
- How you would describe your expectations of that brand.
- What experiences that you have had with the brand have had most impact on you in terms of establishing its reputation?
- Which film or TV star would be a perfect representation of that brand and why?

This little exercise will deepen your appreciation of what makes a powerful brand.

Designing your brand

For the purposes of this subject I put my head together with branding agency Heavenly. Heavenly was created by Richard and Nick Sunderland in 2003. Their approach is to simplify branding so that executives and entrepreneurs can make use of its power with less time and effort than it would take through a conventional process. Heavenly has managed to achieve simplification without losing power or insight. Together with Heavenly I have produced an approach that you can use to design a brand for a consumer company or a business-to-business company, without needing expensive professional help. Here is what you need to do:

1. Identify the central idea behind your brand

Come up with a word or phrase that you most want customers to associate with you. For example, here are some common associations with some famous brands:

- Google: organizing.
- Orange: bright future.
- Apple: design.
- Microsoft: software.
- Firstdirect: 24/7 service.
- Egg: individual money.
- Virgin: consumer champion.
- IBM: global ideas.
- Accenture: performance.

This word is like a design brief for everything you do, say and produce. You are trying to establish that word or phrase in the customer's mind as something that distinguishes you from the crowd.

2. Come up with a promise or a guarantee that the brand offers

Keeping promises is at the heart of a good reputation. Once you are clear what your brand is promising customers each and every time they touch you in any way, you can create a culture that is able to deliver that promise.

Here are some promises associated with some famous brands:

- Google: fast, powerful, ubiquitous, easy-to-use.
- Orange: leading-edge technology that works.
- Apple: gorgeous to look at, beautifully simple and powerful to use.
- Microsoft: comprehensive, feature-rich software that you can rely on.
- Firstdirect: exceptional customer care.
- Egg: enduring good value and use of leading technology.
- Virgin: reliable and enjoyable products and experiences.
- Accenture: delivery to a high standard.

Remember your promises are the benefits I get if I deal with you. Come up with your own promise of benefits. Imagine you have 30 seconds at a dinner party to tell the assembled guests the three benefits of your brand.

3. The brand needs values to bring it to life

Values represent some sort of lifestyle statement or personality. Your culture has to be created with compatible values. (See Chapter 8 for further information on this subject.)

Here are the values I associate with some famous brands:

- Google: super-intelligent, quirky and benign.
- Orange: optimistic, warm and smart.
- Apple: über-cool.
- Microsoft: powerful and aggressive.
- Firstdirect: friendly, helpful and efficient.
- Egg: approachable, quirky and smart.
- Virgin: cool, fun, competent and attractive.
- Accenture: thoroughly professional.

Values are how you would describe your brand if it were person. So imagine the brand is a character (real or fictional). Who would you choose and what are they like? Pick between one and three key values.

4. The brand needs a name

Many companies merely adopt the name of their founder, such as Ford, Dell, Amstrad (A.M. Sugar Trading) and Hewlett-Packard; others use names as a competitive weapon by choosing something distinctive or something that values and reputation can be built around. Such names can be descriptive (Firstdirect, Microsoft or Facebook) or they can be what I call *empty*, such as Egg, Garlik, Apple, Orange and Google. The name is almost irrelevant once a company has become famous and established its reputation, but it's an underused competitive weapon in the early days.

Decide on one of three routes to use:

- your own name
- a descriptive name
- an empty name.

Try brainstorming a dozen possibilities, then pick one you like using your instinct and intuition. When you come to make a final choice, get some professional advice from any reputable firm of lawyers. There are a number of legal and trademark checks you need to make to ensure you are not infringing others' rights.

5. A strong visual identity for a brand is a shortcut to recognition

A strong visual identity acts as a signpost. It triggers almost instantaneous and unambiguous recognition and memory of all of the brand values and promises. Think of any great brand and you'll immediately find that a strong visual identity springs into your mind. It's almost certain you will need some professional help in creating a consistent visual identity for your brand. This need not be at all expensive in the early days. You can find inexpensive freelancers and small local design companies to help you with the artwork or Web and advertising design.

The key thing to remember – and I really want to emphasize this – is to make sure you brief them properly using the brand architecture you should have produced earlier.

6. Brand design needs a reality check

Go back and look at the purpose and goals you created when you wrote the last chapter of your soap opera. Does your brand reflect that purpose?

Look at the ideas for products and services that you created in Chapter 4. Remind yourself of the unmet functional and emotional needs you are targeting. Does the brand architecture reflect this?

Finally, look at everything you have produced – your purpose, the brand, your products and services, and ask yourself whether you can communicate everything in a way that is:

- clear – people will understand what you're offering
- believable – people will believe that what you're offering can be delivered
- credible – people will believe *you* can deliver it
- desirable – it meets currently unmet functional and emotional needs for a segment of consumers or certain types of business
- authentic – the experience of the product or service in action will do what it says on the tin.

You will need to alter something about what you are planning if all of the above conditions are not met.

Communication and sales strategies

Once you have designed a brand, you are ready to tell the world about yourself and your products and services. The way you do this is referred to as a communication strategy. The Internet has transformed marketing communication in recent years, making it plausible for businesses of all sizes to reach a large audience. Whatever sort of business you are creating, it is inconceivable not to have a website these days. It will be a key component in your communication strategy.

You may well need professional help in order to produce a communication strategy. Here is what you need to know to get the best out of any professional you employ. The various means of communication in order of affordability are described below.

Word of mouth

This is also known as viral marketing (because people pass it on to one another). It's a strategy successfully followed by Google,

Facebook, Skype and YouTube. It's quite rare for this to work effectively and quickly on its own but it can often be leveraged by a powerful PR campaign and can be seeded by participation in social networking sites, online communities and by writing a blog.

PR

If you use PR, someone usually has to represent your brand – that person is most likely you. Be prepared for it. Some people are forever associated with brands: Microsoft is Bill Gates, Apple is Steve Jobs, Virgin is Richard Branson and Amstrad is Alan Sugar. I became a part of the brand at Firstdirect and Egg. I deliberately adopted a high profile with all of my ventures; it's much easier for people to relate to a brand if they can identify with the person behind it.

Garlik's CEO, Tom Ilube, is very much a part of the brand, being the personal embodiment of its expertise and insight claims. For any sort of PR campaign, where you are trying to get people to promote your product for free, you need a product (or a stunt or sponsorship deal) that has something unique and exciting about it, certainly for national media. You need a local angle of some sort for regional media. PR was a very powerful weapon for Firstdirect and Egg, and is proving as powerful for Garlik. You almost certainly need a PR agency to get any leverage these days. The media is swamped with companies trying to promote themselves. An agency knows the right journalists, can help craft the right stories and sell them successfully.

Web search

This is where people use the Internet to find you. If you have a product suitable for selling on eBay, you have a ready market of people who might find you. Otherwise it's a matter of understanding the intricacies of Google searches and other means of getting people to find you. This is a complex subject and the domain of specialists, so recruit some professional help.

Affiliates

This refers to paying a website that specializes in referring customers. You pay them a fee for each customer they send you. Getting their attention is hard though because there is huge competition to offer products to successful affiliates. Again, you need professional help for this.

Non-TV advertising: Internet, press, posters, beer mats ...

Display ads come in many different forms and can be placed in infinite locations in order to attract the attention of potential customers. This can be very effective in building awareness but it is no job for an amateur. Writing powerful copy and knowing where and when to place the ads is what professionals are paid for. If you don't have a professional on your team and can't afford to employ a small local agency, don't attempt these ads at all – it can harm your brand if executed poorly. The one exception is ads in local newspapers; if your service is restricted to a local market, these are an inexpensive way to advertise. The newspapers themselves will help you to put an ad together.

Direct marketing

This refers to snail mail or email campaigns and things such as magazine inserts. Email is rarely used to market to large numbers of consumers because you need a list of email addresses of people who have expressed interest in receiving information about products such as yours. Such lists are not easy to obtain and people do not like being spammed – it's illegal as well as irritating. However, business-to-business campaigns or those directed towards existing customers who have given you permission to email are extremely cost-effective.

Large-scale snail mail campaigns are effective for some products but can be very expensive. You need to buy a suitable mailing list, produce the material to be mailed, pay for the envelopes to be addressed and filled, as well as the postage. Despite this it was the most cost-effective means of selling that we found at Firstdirect and, more surprisingly, in the early days at Egg. Later on Egg found that digital marketing overtook direct marketing as a preferred sales route.

Direct marketing to consumers is in decline as people object to junk mail and digital marketing grows in power. It remains effective as a business-to-business tool and when selling a traditional product (such as financial services, wine or clothing) to an existing customer base or anything to a more traditional customer base, such as people who are not active Internet users. A direct marketing campaign needs professional advice – again, seek an inexpensive local marketing agency.

TV advertising campaigns

This is hugely expensive and will be beyond all but the most generously funded new companies. Nonetheless, even in this Internet-driven world it is still the only reliable way to become instantly famous.

Distribution partnerships

Another way to get sales is to partner with a bigger company and leverage their sales capability and their brand. These partnerships are a godsend for a new company if you can get them. You associate yourself with a larger company that gives you instant credibility and sells the product (or a special version of it) for you – keeping some revenue for themselves and giving some to you.

Garlik signed a deal with CPP in September 2007. CPP has ten million customers for its card protection and identity theft products, and gives Garlik a very powerful means of distribution. Egg had partnership deals with Boots and MSN. Google had a deal with AOL that was utterly critical to them in the early days.

Face-to-face selling

If your product is aimed at businesses or you are seeking to develop partnership deals, you need to employ somebody to make calls, knock on doors, open up opportunities, attend trade shows and get sales. Do not stint on paying the right sort of money for such a person and be prepared to put a lot of your own time into it. Indeed, when you start out, it may be only you that does this until you can afford a dedicated salesperson. That's what happened at Garlik – the founders did all this themselves until we could afford to employ a commercial director. Do not underestimate the time it takes to close deals if you are selling face-to-face to big companies. A year from a first conversation to a closed deal is not uncommon.

Do something

Attempt a run-through of the brand design process. You can do this on your own, but involve others if you can. You will end up producing a simple brand architecture similar to the example for Garlik below.

- **The central idea of Garlik**: Illuminating the digital world such that people information and the way it is used is completely transparent to individuals.
- **The brand promise**: We will provide powerful insight into what information is out there about you and what you can and should do about it. We give you control so you feel safer and more empowered.
- **The brand values**: We are the good guys who know how to protect you against the bad guys; Garlik is about people like you.

I'd encourage you even at this stage to try and produce a first cut visual identity as well. Find someone who can sketch – you must know someone. Take them through your brand architecture and ask them to come up with some drawings that dramatize it.

When you come to design your brand for real, you need to go through the design process rigorously with your team. You can find inexpensive professional help if you need it – type 'marketing agency or marketing consultant' into an Internet search engine and look for freelancers or small local companies. You can get help to produce your advertising promotion and search campaign in the same way.

8

Creating a powerful culture

'Though this be madness, yet there is method in't.'

William Shakespeare, *Hamlet* (Act II, Scene 2)

Business culture concerns how you create a working environment that delivers your brand promise to your employees and in turn your customers. It affects the speed and quality of everything your company does and also what's possible for your company. As far as I'm concerned, your culture is one of your few key weapons against the established giants that will be trying to crush you.

Many large companies suppress people's natural motivation and creativity in order to keep a tight control on how things are done and how money is spent. Decisions and subsequent actions move along at a sloth's pace, caught up in a tight net of bureaucracy. As Sir Peter Davis, then CEO of Prudential and Chairman of Egg, said to me just after the launch of Egg in 1998: 'It sounds like you have just more than doubled your call centre capacity in four days. It would take them four days to find the right forms in Pru.'

Fortunately, in their early days new companies rarely suffer from the same draining bureaucratic problems. In fact, escaping the quagmire of the average corporate culture is a key motivator for many people who start their own business.

> *'In 1995, having survived 16 interviews to get into the world's best investment bank, Goldman Sachs, and after two hectic and successful years in the job, I reached a sudden and personally shocking realization – I was in the wrong place. The famously powerful and driven company culture was just wrong for me. I wanted more freedom for myself and my soul. I therefore created my own company – Lost Wax – not only because I wanted to escape someone else's corporate culture, but because I wanted to work in a place where I would be surrounded by diverse, relaxed, free-thinking people and I could wear a woolly jumper.'*

Tom Ilube, founder of software company Lost Wax and Garlik CEO

However, if you don't give some attention to culture right from the start, you definitely miss an opportunity to create a long-term competitive advantage. In order to harness this, you have to start to create a culture from the very first day of the company's existence – this chapter tells you how.

In my experience, entrepreneurs need a lot of convincing about the power of culture – and yet I believe that, when well-executed, it can be an immensely valuable asset. The difficult thing is for me to convince you to take it seriously, because what you have to do to ensure a successful culture in the early days of a new company is actually very easy. The majority of my advice on this subject might sound like common sense, but it's still extremely rare that people pay adequate attention to this fundamental aspect of their business in the beginning. Perhaps your ears might prick up if I told you that it is one of the easiest ways to give yourself an instant advantage over your established competitors.

In my companies I've always given huge priority to creating a culture where people felt it was safe to bring their humanity to work with them. I've always encouraged my colleagues to express themselves without worrying about how they looked. I reinforced that rather dramatically at Mercury by turning up at work dressed as King Arthur and having members of the management team dressed as Merlin and the knights of the Round Table. It certainly got everybody's attention, signalling the fact that things were changing and that management means what it says – worry more about expressing yourself than how you look.

Dressed in a robe and crown, I told people to worry about being extraordinary – not about looking good or being politically correct. Accepting fallibility and honest mistakes helped avoid a culture of blame when things did go wrong. We just got on with fixing the problem, honouring those with the courage to get on the pitch and give it their all – win or lose.

As a result of this approach and many other cultural initiatives in Mercury and elsewhere, I was rewarded with what all human beings have to offer: wisdom, courage, commitment, resilience, creativity, stupidity, anger and more besides. You can't have one without the other – everyone is a flawed genius in one dimension or another. Unleashing genius more than compensates for having to deal with those flaws. It translates into a competitive edge in terms of the speed and quality of response to opportunities and threats.

The notion of putting so much effort into creating a culture when you are just starting out (particularly creating a culture that liberates the full range of human emotions and behaviours) may sound like madness. But I can assure you – and hopefully convince you – that there is method in it. Creating a powerful culture is an important priority from the very first few breaths of your organization.

Every organization has a culture

It might sound odd to talk about 'culture' when it comes to creating a new business. Often there are only a handful of you – maybe as few as two or three. But somewhat surprisingly, it's relevant to all organizations, large and small, new and old.

Culture exists in any company that has more than one person; it exists in the tiny Pukka Herbs just as much as it exists in the giant Virgin Group.

I've heard many definitions of organizational culture. It's often referred to as the organization's DNA, which is a good analogy. Personally I relate to culture as a mixture of the following:

- What's important in this organization?
- Who's important?
- How are things done around here?
- What does it take to get on here?
- What are the unwritten rules that seem to be in operation here?

Do something

Think of an organization you know well. Try and describe the culture in terms of the questions I have listed above. When you are thinking about the unwritten rules, it can be helpful to think about them in terms of: what is considered politically correct here?

This exercise can reveal for the first time what culture actually is and give people a real sense of its power.

Conversations about these topics happen at every level of an organization or project, whatever its size and age. This is how people come to conclusions about the culture. It happens at lightning speed and solidifies just as quickly, independent of its nature. Once people have drawn conclusions about those questions, they become as solid a reality for everyone as the office walls. No one questions them – that's just the way things are.

If you don't actively manage the creation of a culture, then you get what I call a *default culture*. In a new company this will be based on the personalities of the founders and other key people who join. It is a matter of chance whether such a culture helps or hinders your cause. What's worse is that as the company grows, the ability of a few dominant personalities to control the culture fades. The default culture then starts to approach the bureaucratic nightmare that permeates many large companies.

'The initial DNA of the company is very hard to change, so it is imperative to get it right from the outset.'

Brent Hoberman, co-founder of Lastminute.com

Changing an already established culture is challenging, to say the least. It is incredibly easy to find examples of this situation.

The US telephone giant AT&T, founded in the 19th century and employing a million people at its peak, attempted a fundamental transformation when the new CEO Michael Armstrong arrived in 1997. The cautious and classically politically correct culture of AT&T, which was led by engineering and research, was to be transformed into one supporting a 'telecoms supermarket' for the digital age. Major acquisitions of cable TV and mobile assets supported this strategy, but it failed. By 2005, AT&T no longer existed as an independent company. It has been broken up and the parts acquired by companies that were never as powerful as AT&T was at its peak.

Sir Peter Bonfield took over as CEO at BT in 1996. He fell on his sword in 2001 having failed to shift the BT culture sufficiently to match his ambitions of building a global, competitive telecoms company.

In July 1999, Hewlett-Packard appointed Carly Fiorina as CEO. Fiorina was the first woman ever to serve as CEO of a company included in the Dow Jones Industrial Average.

On 9 February 2005, Carly Fiorina was dismissed as chairman and CEO. In the years between, she wrestled with a culture that had hardly changed since the company was established in 1947 by founders Bill Hewlett and Dave Packard. HP is a Silicon Valley institution – in fact, its establishment created Silicon Valley.

Today it is the biggest technology vendor in the world, but when Fiorina took over it was struggling. No one had been able to pick up the mantle of the founders after they had retired. The culture they established – an obsession with innovation, quality and perfectionism, together with an informal family-like atmosphere and job security for life – was the source of HP's success.

Indeed, the founders used to say that 'the company exists to make technical contributions for the advancement and welfare of humanity'.

Fiorina saw that the culture needed to change in order to cope with global competition and compete with upstarts like Dell. She pushed through an unpopular merger with Compaq, seeing complementary technical skills in the two companies: Compaq was strong on PCs and Windows-based software, HP strong on servers and Unix-based software. But to a business customer such as me, the cultures clashed horribly. HP's intellectual focus on innovation met Compaq's aggressive sales culture and the result was discordance.

Fiorina tried to get HP to lower its perfectionist standards using a slogan of 'perfect enough' – in other words, there's a time when further focus on design excellence, robustness and quality gives diminishing returns.

She also dismantled the 'jobs for life' policy, outsourced work offshore and announced significant redundancies. The opposition to all of this was led by the founders' children, Walter Packard and David Wooley Packard.

At the time it was hard not to feel sorry for her – she must have felt like she was in the middle of a nightmare.

Her replacements didn't last long and further turmoil followed until current CEO Mark Hurd took over in late 2006. He seems to have set the company back on track, helped by the growing popularity of laptops (where HP is strong) and by the troubles at Dell.

Getting your culture right from the outset

I hope I've started to convince you to put some effort into getting your culture right from day one. Its one thing to try and change it when you have become a giant company – that's something most have to face eventually – but you don't want to have to take that on in the early years of your new company.

Getting culture right from the outset is exactly what Google founders Larry Page and Sergey Brin achieved, as did Richard Branson with Virgin – they both gave huge priority to creating cultures that acted as a powerful asset.

But possibly the best example of the powerful and resilient nature of a culture is provided by Steve Jobs. As a co-founder of Apple back in 1976, he suffered the same fate as many founders when he was forced out of the company in 1985 after a clash with then CEO John Scully. Jobs went on to found another computer company called NeXt and exploded into the film business through his creation of the computer animation business Pixar, which was responsible for blockbusters such as *Toy Story*, *Finding Nemo* and *The Incredibles*.

Jobs was flourishing, but by 1997 Apple had got itself into dire straits. It desperately needed new software and purchased Jobs' new company NeXt to get it. Jobs returned to Apple as CEO as part of the deal. And in doing so, he found the culture he had originally created had ossified and deteriorated in his absence – the fire had gone out. It had become as bureaucratic as any other large company and Apple, which lived on enthusiasm and innovation, was on its knees as a result.

> *'It was much worse than I could imagine. The people have been told they were losers for so long. There were on the verge of giving up. The first six months was very bleak and at times I got close to throwing in the towel too.'*

Steve Jobs, taken from Young, 2006

Jobs experienced the extreme difficulty of changing a culture (even back to what it used to be) first hand. He did succeed eventually and of course the rest is history: the iPod, iTunes, the iMac and related innovations have transformed a dying company into a powerhouse. Soaring product sales, a growing reputation and high investor expectations sent Apple's stock into the stratosphere. Incredibly, the company's value overtook that of technology giant IBM in November 2007.

Culture is created the second you begin to communicate

Hopefully, all this evidence will go some way towards convincing you of the importance of culture, as well as its resilience once established. As I mentioned previously, in the absence of an explicit culture creation programme, it grows in relation to how the founders react to circumstances that the organization encounters in its early days. The organization watches the founders obsessively, and quickly comes to some conclusions about what it's really like here.

This process actually starts the very first time you open your mouth to say anything. How you react and what you say in your organization therefore determines whether people:

- feel it's safe to challenge you or just do as they are told
- trust you and believe that you are honest and authentic about what you say
- feel it's safe to take risks and whether you'll be by their side supporting them if they get into difficulties
- feel it's safe to be human or whether it's safer to suppress their essential humanity in favour of adopting an occupational persona.

After a while these questions cease to be about you and become about the way things are in your organization. Conclusions about what's important, how things are done and what it takes to get on become set in stone. So unless you explicitly create and manage the cultural conversations that exist in the organization from its very earliest days, you end up with a default culture that grows by chance, but almost always leans towards cynical bureaucracy.

Back to enthusiasm … again!

A powerful culture is one where everyone in the organization is enthusiastic about the company and fundamentally believes in delivering the brand promise. These companies are remarkable and few. As well as Apple, Virgin and Google, I can think of Microsoft, 3M, Nokia, Toyota, GE, Starbucks, Innocent and Samsung, and maybe a handful of others – then I get stuck. Notably, the power of these cultures was established in the earliest days of the company.

When I listen to executives at Apple, Virgin and Google, I hear people who display a natural enthusiasm for their company and its products. Perhaps even more impressive is that wherever you come across the employees of these companies, at any level in the organization, they are equally enthusiastic. Expressing that enthusiasm is an important part of delivering the brand promise.

At Google, people are passionate about creative uses of information. Their engineers are actually expected to spend 20% of their time creating and developing new ideas – ideas that they are enthusiastic about and that support the brand promise of organizing the world's information.

As I write this, I've just got off a Virgin Atlantic flight from New York. Every member of the cabin crew seemed to enjoy their time on that flight and infected the passengers with that sense of enjoyment. That's great for Virgin, whose brand promise is centred on fun and entertainment.

Every time I meet someone from Apple, they are quick to overwhelm me with an enthusiastic advocacy of their products. It's a consistent pitch: the design of their product, and how easily and effectively they work. And what's Apple's brand promise? An iconic design that's easy to use and looks great.

I get the sense that people in all of these companies are acknowledged, appreciated and rewarded for expressing their enthusiasm in line with the company's unique vision and delivering its brand promise.

I previously spoke about the power of infecting everybody with your own enthusiasm in the context of taking the initial first steps towards your Bold and Inspiring Future. Well, liberating enthusiasm is just as powerful in driving the business forward as it is in getting started in the first place.

All large organizations have an element of bureaucracy about them. The best ones, however, retain an enthusiasm that allows them to continue to be innovative and inspiring places to work even as they grow.

Worst-case scenario

The worst kind of default culture is where people's natural spirit is censored in the name of conformity, governance, health and safety, codes of conduct, controls, targets, and political correctness. These are organizations where, for those who work in them, fear of failure dominates. Trying to look good to those who measure them with arbitrary and meaningless targets becomes more important than doing the right thing, taking responsibility or being creative. If you allow the dreaded default culture to grow, then one thing is certain – it will choke your business before it can reach anything like its full potential.

Be big without bureaucracy

The bigger and more successful the business gets, the more important culture becomes. Large companies often grow through innovation. But quite often, the more successful they get, the worse they become at bringing new ideas to life. Ideas flourish in an environment characterized by urgency, creativity, powerful expressions of the human spirit and risk-taking. Bureaucratic companies stay successful by controlling things; they don't like disruptive influences. People don't rise to the top by delivering the set of small failures that almost always provide important lessons for successful innovation. For these reasons, bureaucratic companies can become vulnerable to competitive attacks from newcomers and are not well-equipped to seize new opportunities.

On the other hand, a successful company such as Apple, which has grown spectacularly since Jobs returned while retaining a culture of innovation, is very powerful indeed. In fact, it's such a powerful force that Apple was able to snatch leadership of the music industry away from Sony, which created the Walkman, established record labels and had a massive consumer electronics business. How on earth did Apple do that?

The answer is a partly powerful culture and partly great leadership on the part of Jobs. The Apple culture that he reinvented in 1997 was critically important. It turned out to be a powerful long-term competitive advantage.

> *'Apple literally was failing when Steve went back and re-infused the innovation and risk-taking that have been phenomenal'*
>
> Bill Gates

So how did Jobs set about revitalizing the Apple culture and what can we learn from that?

Primarily, he communicated incessantly about what he believed in and what he was going to make happen both inside and outside the company.

He made it incredibly clear what he believed in:

- design excellence
- a status-free organization, with no special treatment for executives
- winning and sharing the rewards of success
- loyalty.

He told everyone: 'Everything's going to be different here from now on – you are either with me or you can go.'

This whole message was reinforced by posters everywhere featuring the message 'Think Different' – this encapsulated Job's whole approach.

Jobs also backed up his words with actions. He got rid of most of the board and many senior executives, replacing them with people who saw the world in the same way as he did:

- He instituted widespread bonus and share schemes linked to company success.
- He banned business class travel.
- He banned talking to the press, a route Apple executives had come to regard as the best way to express dissent.
- Most importantly of all, he held regular product review meetings where he hammered home the importance of paying adequate attention to the core Apple value of design excellence.

So in a nutshell that's how you create a culture: you communicate incessantly about your beliefs and intentions and you match your words with strong actions. You reinforce your beliefs with an evident intolerance for people, behaviours and designs that don't support your view of the world.

And it seems he was successful:

> *'Apple employees all like one another, and they have a strong
> sense that they are the chosen of the Earth, and they're not going
> to be a jerk about it, but all others who dwell on this mortal coil
> are missing out by not working here.'*

Lev Grossman, *Time* magazine, 24 October 2005

Easy to implement

So in summary, here is how you implement a powerful culture in a new company. As you will see, it's mostly common sense:

- Talk to people about what you are up to, what your brand promise is all about and what that means they must do.
- Listen with proper attention to what they say in response.
- Talk only about what you really believe in.
- Ensure your actions match your words.
- Show appreciation for people, attitudes, behaviours and designs that support the brand promise and express intolerance for anything that doesn't.
- Employ people who see the world the way you do, give them space to be themselves and create a workplace where people enjoy coming to work – a place where you would be happy to work yourself if you weren't the owner.

'We produce a communications pack every month and the whole company meets every Monday for 30 minutes for a quick update. We have more extensive shindigs every quarter and a big gathering once a year. Everybody in Innocent joins a house (we have 12), which is like a social network and helps people settle in.

'We want to create a business we can be proud of. We want Innocent to become a global, natural, ethical food company, always remaining commercially successful and socially aware. To make this happen, we need brilliant people, who inspire and deliver change all around them. So that's why we're always looking for talented, ambitious and altruistic folks to come and join us.

'Our style is to work hard and to make sure that everyone gets to share in the upside. To give people the opportunity to develop themselves and each other, and to reward them when they do so. And to bake everyone a homemade cake on their birthday. It's an approach that's led to us being awarded The Best Workplace in the UK by both The Guardian and The National Business Awards, along with a whole selection of other awards. And we intend to make it even better.'

Richard Reed, co-founder, Innocent Drinks

As your company grows, other issues such as the working environment, training and coaching, remuneration structures, performance reviews, career development, approval processes, and IT systems start to become critical to culture. By the time you get that big, you will be able to afford an HR professional who can take care of all of that for you, but in the early days, communicating consistently, clearly and authentically is the most important thing to focus on.

The culture at Egg

People who visited the Egg offices would often say 'Wow, this place is really buzzing.'

I was always extremely pleased to hear it. As CEO, I tried to create a culture that remained innovative long after the launch of our first product. This took a huge amount of communication, attention to recruitment, training and of course a lot of attention on treating our employees exactly the way we expected them to treat customers – as individuals.

We had a young team at the time. And some people had questioned their ability to pull off something as ambitious as Egg. But I told them:

> *'I'm backing this team; your job is to play the game full on without fear of failure. It's not to win at all costs. We'll keep our eye on the score board to guide us, not as the be all and end all.'*

I spoke to Christine Hayes, who was Director of Credit and Risk at Egg, recently. I asked her for her impressions of her time at Egg.

> *'Egg was a lovely company, an extraordinary company whichever way you looked at it and wherever you touched it. It was full of humour, energy, human frailty, human courage and human genius. It also had the merit of never taking itself too*

seriously. We knew at the end of the day it really was all just a game, which was incredibly liberating.'

As I mentioned before, Egg powered on to become the fastest ever growing UK bank and the biggest Internet bank in the world. It grew to be worth £1.3bn in less than two years.

The culture was an important part of that. I put a strong emphasis on ensuring that Egg had a culture that could deliver the brand promise of giving customers a stunning and individual experience. If we could make this happen, then we would have achieved no less than a revolution in customers' experience of financial services. Our starting point was generating passion for that revolution in our employees. This took all of the things I outlined earlier: communication, matching words with actions, appreciation for attitudes and actions that supported the brand promise, and intolerance for anything which didn't.

What you actually need to do is common sense. Making sure you give it enough attention is the key.

You will soon find out for yourself that creating a desirable culture in the early days of an organization is simple and free of charge. All you have to do is communicate one-to-one to each new person who joins your team. Later, as your company grows, you will have to communicate to whole groups of new people and follow the advice I gave you earlier in this chapter. Telling people what the company is about and how things are done is the most critical aspect of establishing a culture that meets the brand promise. Do this consistently and at every opportunity, and of course demonstrate what you say in the actions you take.

Do something

What I want you to do now is write the speech that you will use to rally the troops at every opportunity.

The speech needs to:

- educate people about the company and the brand you are creating
- show people what role they can play to make a real difference
- explain how your brand values will show up in the way that everybody behaves in the organization.

Below is the speech that Tom Ilube gave to rally the troops in the early days of Garlik – it might help to inspire you.

'This company is going to be a global phenomenon. We will take the best of emerging technology, the next generation of the Web itself – the Semantic Web – to give individuals and their families real power over their personal information in the digital world. We have placed ourselves in customer's shoes in designing this company – we are on the customers' side.

'We will recognize people are individuals, every digital identity is different and every customer is different. We will try and make all of our products and all of our communications with customers responsive to their individual needs. Every step a customer takes in the digital world leaves a footprint and every customer has a unique footprint. We will walk side by side along the path that our customers want to follow as they explore the amazing world of the Internet.

'We will treat our colleagues as individuals too. We want you to discover and grow confident in your own individuality here. We want you to know what that feels like so you can deliver the same experience to our customers. We want you to feel powerful here, to explore, to express yourself and to be unleashed. We want you to be able to tell your friends and family this is an

extraordinary place to work. You didn't think workplaces like this existed. You will have a great time here and be well rewarded but we need you to work your socks off as well – that's a fair deal, isn't it?

'Let me tell you about our brand – we think of it as a promise – a promise to give people insight in dealing with their personal information, a set of benefits all of which boil down to this: with Garlik you get a set of simple and effective solutions to help you protect and promote your personal information in the digital world, and a set of values – these are about being on the customer's side and about powerful insight – showing customers what's really going on and what really matters.

'Then there's the name, of course. Instantly memorable and a bit shocking for an identity company. That should get us some attention in a crowded world. We've used elegant design to have the brand show up as smart and powerful. Elegant Garlik has nothing to do with spice, vampires or bad breadth – you won't stink of garlic here, this Garlik is powerful stuff and it's good for you too.

'Our first job and the one I want to engage you in is to launch in November with no compromise to our principles and with the website getting hammered by potential customers. Leave me to worry about profit – your job is to be yourselves and give the customers what we promise. That's what it takes to get on here.'

You will find yourself giving this sort of speech over and over, until the culture of the company is exactly as you want it and becomes almost invisible to everyone on the inside. It may not be a tangible aspect of your business but that doesn't make it any less powerful.

Also, make sure that when you produce your initial dynamic action plan that someone has accountability for creating and establishing the brand and that you take personal responsibility for creating a culture that reflects the brand values.

Few new businesses give brand and culture enough attention and that, together with over-optimism about cash flow, is the main reason so many fail in my opinion.

Give yourself an edge – make brand and a matching culture a personal priority!

9

Leadership and the edge of reason

'Reasonable people adapt themselves to the world. Unreasonable people attempt to adapt the world to themselves. All progress, therefore, depends on unreasonable people.'

George Bernard Shaw

Imagine you have already started your new business: you've got the funds in the bank and most of your planning and design work has been done. Your job is now to lead the business through the first 12 months using the three documents you will have produced – the plan of action, the brand design and the speech about your culture.

The principles of leadership are the same whether you are a small start-up struggling to maintain existence in its first 12 months or a five-year-old viable business powering confidently ahead.

The fundamental principle of leadership: maintaining a precarious balance on the edge of reason

I think it's safe to say that most people are rational and reasonable about most things, most of the time. Of course, effective leaders are rational and reasonable too, but not about most things and not most of the time. People might like effective leaders, they might hate them, they might even love them – but the word they will most often use to describe them is unreasonable.

You see, to be an effective leader you need to maintain an almost irrational belief that ultimately you will reach the Bold and Inspiring Future that you have designed, and at the same time be ruthlessly honest with yourself and others about where you are today.

In the early days of your business there will be a huge gap between your current position and your ultimate destination. It is a leader's job to make sure that no one is discouraged by the scale of this gap. In addition to the daunting chasm between where you are now and the future that you are committed to, there will be times when things just aren't working: your results are disappointing, you are not making sufficient progress and the gap seems to be getting wider.

It is a leader's job to help everyone to be ruthlessly honest about what isn't working, while steering them away from the obvious rational conclusion – 'we are not good enough'.

You need to adopt the apparently unreasonable attitude that your past performance is no indication of what you are capable of in the future. Most rational people would take the opposite view.

Being a leader can put you in a very uncomfortable position. You have to be simultaneously rational about the present and somewhat irrational about the future and the past – often in the same sentence. This position is balanced precariously on the very edge of reason.

The Iron Lady

Love her or loathe her, Margaret Thatcher was responsible for a huge transformation in the UK's economic fortune: from the sick man of Europe to a vibrant enterprise economy. It was a transformation considered impossible by every previous post-war Prime Minister.

It was actually quite reasonable to believe that such a transformation wasn't possible. Just before the Thatcher government came to power, senior civil servants were quoted in *The Sunday Times* saying that 'Britain's decline is inevitable, our job is to make that process as civilized as possible'.

I met Baroness Thatcher in 1999 at a party given to celebrate her retirement as Chancellor of Buckingham University. The new Chancellor, Sir Martin Jacomb, had commissioned a portrait of her to commemorate her time at Buckingham. Just before the portrait was unveiled, Baroness Thatcher asked me about Egg – how we had chosen the name and how far I thought we could push Internet banking. She was not chatting politely; she was actually asking me more challenging questions than I usually got from the Egg board. Denis, however, was looking bored and was concentrating on his gin and tonic, probably hoping to get back to the conversation on golf we had been having previously.

Then the portrait was unveiled and Denis muttered something unintelligible. The portrait was definitely not flattering. Baroness Thatcher stared at it for a while in silence and then turned to the press and said:

'I like that. That's a portrait of a powerful woman. And we were a powerful woman! We had strong principles, principles of freedom, principles of enterprise ...'

She went on to make a great impromptu speech. It was a powerful pitch from one of the most unreasonable people I have ever met. She was unreasonable in her expectations and her demands on people. She was unreasonable in her determination to make things happen whatever obstacles she encountered and however many people told her what she was doing was impossible. She was unreasonable in her support of the people who worked with her. She was unreasonable in refusing to accept that past failures meant the future could not be different.

I still remember a speech she made in 1980. She was under fire from all sides, including her own party, after less than a year in power. The general consensus was that like every Prime Minister before her who had tried to reinvigorate the British economy with hard and radical policies, she would soon be forced into a U-turn. She responded to this notion with magnificent defiance: 'You turn if you want to. The lady's not for turning.'

Not only was this reply unreasonable but it was also irrational given the circumstances she was facing and the amount of opposition to her policies. And yet, if you listened to her give an analysis of the global and local issues facing the UK, you would conclude this was a person with a complete and totally rational grip on the issues of the day.

She was rational about the present; unreasonable about the future she was committed to and unwilling to take the apparently reasonable and rational view that past failures (hers and other people's) meant something.

Whatever your political views and whatever you thought of the direction she took the country in, please accept that what she did demonstrate, without any doubt, was effective leadership.

'She was a tigress surrounded by hamsters.'

John Biffen, 'The revenge of the unburied dead', *The Observer*, 9 December 1990

'The Prime Ministers who are remembered are those who think and teach, and not many do. Mrs. Thatcher ... influenced the thinking of a generation.'

Tony Benn, quoted in Peter Hennessy, 2001

'Her strong points were her iron will. I've never known a will like it in politics and I've known a few politicians in my time in various countries. I've never known a man or woman faintly like her, she was as tough as they come, and anything that required guts and will she could do for you.'

Brian Walden, *Westminster Hour*, BBC

Who needs leadership anyway?

> *Do something*
>
> When I run seminars on leadership, I normally start by asking the participants to consider a few basic questions:
>
> - Why isn't a hotel manager called a hotel leader?
> - Why is the G8 summit of Presidents and Prime Ministers called a leadership summit, not a management summit?
> - Why is a leader necessary and in what circumstances?
> - What does a leader do?
>
> Whatever answers you came up with, it's generally easy to see that leading the implementation of a new idea and/or the creation of a new company is all about change. Starting with nothing, you have to implement massive changes in order to arrive at the Bold and Inspiring Future you have designed. To do this effectively, you have to stay balanced on the edge of reason as I have described.

One of the hardest things to get used to when you are leading a new company is how out of control everything seems to feel. At times it seems like a crazy hustle as everything appears to conspire to unbalance you.

I have just watched, for the first time in years, a video that we made at Egg at the end of 1999. People at all levels in the organization were interviewed and one after another they said: 'It's been like a rollercoaster.'

If people all over the organization feel that way, imagine how it must feel for the leader. It's often a matter of hanging on for dear life as you whiz down the dips, around the corners and soar up the other side.

I have often watched seemingly out-of-control events swirl around me and during these white knuckle rides I found it extremely helpful to remember it was all just a soap opera. I remember thinking exactly that in the middle of one of Egg's crises, where we were trying to deal with the overwhelming demand for one of our products. I was completely focused on making sure we had everything in place to deal with all the potential customer issues we faced and then I turned my attention to discussing my forthcoming TV interrogation with our PR advisors.

I missed the fact that a bunch of animal rights activists were marching towards our building – Prudential, which owned the offices, was a target for some reason. I had a temporary PA at the time who had only been in the office for a couple of days. We had barely spoken. She had been briefed on the likely tactics of the activists if they got into the offices and panicked when she heard the chants of the protesters as they marched towards us. She came into my office and said without preamble 'If a group of naked women come into your office, try not to let them touch you and whatever you do keep your hands off them.' Then she marched out again without another word.

I suppose I looked mildly puzzled. I'd learned not to be fazed by anything that Egg could throw at me by then. Being confronted by the entire range of human behaviour is one not entirely beneficial side-effect of liberating the human spirit at work. The external PR advisors who were relatively new to Egg did seem a tad perturbed by the incident and kept at least half an eye on the door for a while. The internal Egg PR dealt with it briskly enough. Like me, she was used to dealing with the unexpected and the inexplicable without letting it distract her from her main purpose.

As Harold Macmillan said, 'The problem with leadership is events, dear boy, events.' Random and unexpected events come at you from all angles, seemingly determined to knock you off your perch and either topple you over into complete delusion or drag you back into total rationality. Either place is bad. If you allow yourself to be deluded about where you are now, you are likely to have a disaster. If you are not clear where you are in a storm, you have no chance of choosing a sensible direction to move in and you are quite likely to walk off the edge of a cliff. Most corporate and public policy disasters result from delusions about the way things are now.

Many entrepreneurs I've spoken to think along the same lines. Five examples come up consistently:

- Cable & Wireless's recycling of the cash it had generated from the sale of assets such as Mercury and Hong Kong Telecom into overpriced Internet assets in 1999–2000. From outside the company, it was obvious to many that while a long-term strategy of supplying telecom infrastructure for the Internet made sense, the company seemed deluded about *the way things are now*. The overcapacity in the market meant that Cable & Wireless were swapping cash for worthless assets and so the share price fell from more than £15 to less than £1.
- The almost identical story at Marconi, where observers watched in fascinated horror at the prices being paid for what turned out to be worthless assets; Marconi seemed so seduced by a bold long-term strategy to be a leader in the technology that powered the Internet that they became deluded about *the way things are now* in the telecoms market and they barely survived at all.
- Another example is Enron. Not the company itself, which was guilty of fraud rather than delusion, but all of the investment banks who queued up to help Enron structure its dubious off-balance sheet companies, which hid the true state of the company's finances. The banks seemed mesmerized by the power of Enron's reputation and long-term vision – it was voted America's most innovative and admired Company by *Fortune* magazine for every year between 1966 and 2000. As a consequence

the banks deluded themselves about *where Enron is now* and why it needed so many unusual (and what often turned out to be illegal) financial structures.

- The long-term vision of the US neocons to create a series of western-style democracies in the Middle East, starting in Iraq, can be criticized – but that was not the source of the disaster. Failure to plan how to deal with the chaotic situation on the ground after the invasion caused the initial trouble and then a continuing assertion by politicians that 'things were getting better', when everyone on the ground knew they were getting worse, turned a problem into a disaster. Once more a delusion about *the way things are now* was the source of the problem.

- I've heard many people who work within the National Health Service say the government is completely deluded about the actual state of play. The politicians say that things are improving – this does not, apparently, reflect *the way things are now.* The reality is that morale in the NHS is worse than it has ever been.

I hope these examples help you appreciate that you have to be totally realistic about *the way things are now* if you are to avoid disaster. On the other hand, if you get too rational about the future you will start to get trapped by how difficult it all seems and you are likely to paralyse everything with over-caution.

The key leadership lesson I have drawn from my own experience is that you need to stay focused on your goal of a Bold and Inspiring Future whatever circumstances you are facing today. You also need to communicate a comforting confidence to all around you. Even if events blow you wildly off course, you are constantly saying to yourself and others: 'Look – here's where we are. We know where we are headed. We'll get there a step at a time. Here's the next step – let's do it now.'

The most potent example of leadership like this that I have come across is not someone starting a new company, it comes from someone determined to make his idea happen.

Peter Darbee is Chairman of Pacific Gas and Electric (PG&E). He is transforming what was a sleepy, unloved California energy utility into a world leader in green energy. I've mentioned PG&E previously but here I want to focus on Peter's leadership approach.

PG&E Corporation is a $34bn energy-based holding company that owns Pacific Gas and Electric Company, one of the largest combination natural gas and electric utilities in the United States. The utility serves 15 million people throughout a 70,000 square mile service area in northern and central California.

Since Peter Darbee took charge of PG&E on 1 January 2005, he has undertaken a thorough transformation of a once bureaucratic and slow-moving utility with a reputation for poor customer service.

Peter's idea was to create an energy company that would be a leader in the fight to combat climate change, while also continuing to do a great job for its shareholders. It's hard to think of a more challenging idea or one that could potentially benefit so many of us.

When Peter first made his idea public at the Prestigious Keystone Center Leadership awards dinner, where he was receiving an award, the MC (Kokie Roberts) said: 'Did I just hear what I heard?' Peter wasn't taking the orthodox US energy utility position, to the surprise and delight of all environmentalists.

In driving PG&E forward within this overarching context, Peter set a short-term focus on five objectives and under his stewardship the current performance of PG&E has already been transformed:

- **Customer centricity:** 30% to 65% customer approval.
- **Operational excellence:** JD Powers fourth quartile to first quartile rating. (JD Powers is an agency that publishes ratings of large companies based on customer satisfaction data and an assessment of the quality and efficiency of the company's processes.)
- **Regulator alignment:** From conflict to admiration, with regulators stating 'We are proud of what this company has become.'
- **Environmental leadership:** A pledge to get 20% of energy from renewable sources by 2010 puts them in the leading one or two US utilities and ahead of anything the UK is likely to achieve.
- **Earnings growth:** Flat to 7.5% pa.

On his longer-term objective, Peter is active with other business leaders (in a CEO roundtable) and politicians in trying to create the right regulatory structure and incentives to enable business to take a lead and show the way to combat climate change.

On 18 October 2006, *The San Francisco Chronicle* reported: *'Environmental activists give Darbee credit for focusing PG&E on increased use of renewable energy and for becoming vocal on the need for businesses to take a more dynamic role in addressing the problem of climate change.*

'"What he's talking about is very welcome," said Carl Zichella, California regional director for the Sierra Club (an environmental pressure group). "It's important to have business leaders of his calibre talking about this."'

Peter worked with his entire leadership team to create their Bold and Inspiring Future – as compelling a vision as I have seen since Kennedy.

'The game we are playing goes beyond our company, our industry and our country. We are reshaping the way energy impacts people's lives around the world. We will create the model utility, we will serve customers in a safe and environmentally sustainable manner, and transform our industry by reshaping the technology and infrastructure to supply and deliver green energy. We will enable the unthinkable, creating energy products and services which are tailored to customers' preferred lifestyle, inspiring customers to make responsible energy-saving choices, achieving breakthroughs in energy efficiency, conservation and levels of demand. We will ensure secure and affordable energy supply, production and delivery, raising the bar on environmental stewardship and enriching the communities where our customers and employees live and work. By doing this we will energize our employees and reward our shareholders.'

Peter Darbee

Peter's approach to leadership displays a perfect example of balancing on the edge of reason:

'You have to radiate confidence about getting somewhere, despite the fact you don't know how to get there. You have to be prepared to be thought crazy as I was when I said we were going to be the best in the world when people thought we were about the worst. The best leaders are tough, pragmatic drivers who make apparently crazy promises. People love them.'

Peter Darbee

While clearly heading for his Bold and Inspiring Future with initiatives inside and outside his industry, he has not neglected the facts of his current reality. And he has focused very much on meeting short-term performance goals while never losing sight of or faith in his long-term vision.

The painstaking academic research of Jim Collins and his 21-strong research team also illustrates the importance of facing facts in order to be a successful leader. Jim began as an academic at the Stanford Graduate School of Business and is now a management researcher, guru and writer. In his book *Good to Great*, Jim concludes that the most effective leaders display what he calls *the Stockdale paradox*:

> US Admiral James Stockdale survived for eight years as a prisoner of war in Vietnam, whereas most people lasted less than a year, and said of his ordeal: 'You must never confuse faith that you will prevail in the end – which you can never afford to lose – with the discipline to confront the most brutal facts of your current reality, whatever they might be.'

Collins' advice to leaders is almost word for word what Stockdale said:

'Retain absolute faith that you can and will prevail in the end, regardless of the difficulties, AND at the same time confront the most brutal facts of your current reality, whatever they might be.'

Leadership in action

Well I hope you understand the sort of attitude you will need to adopt to become an effective leader. Next we'll take a look at what you actually need *to do* to lead the company through those first critical 12 months using the plan of action, the brand design and the culture-creating speech.

There are six things that only the leader can do. The key leadership accountabilities are:

1. Regularly recreating an empowering culture.
2. Creating the 'power gap'.
3. Preparing for competition.
4. Watching the cash.
5. Choosing the risks you take and those you don't.
6. Creating a hot leadership team.

1. Regularly recreating an empowering culture

You need to keep telling everyone in your organization, including yourself, where you are going (both by the end of this 12 month period and your ultimate destination) and why, what you believe in and why, and where you are now and what that means. Use the culture-creating speech you produced in Chapter 8 for this and make sure you update it from time to time to take account of what's happening.

2. Creating the Power Gap

Leaders need to continually create what I call *the power gap*. This is the gap between what you are committed to achieving in the future and your totally honest and rational assessment of the way things are today.

I call it the power gap because it's designed to empower people to choose actions that fill this gap. You will need to regularly create a power gap for each condition of satisfaction in your dynamic action plan:

1 Take each condition of satisfaction in your plan and break it down into milestones – monthly or quarterly, depending on the condition. Milestones define what must be achieved by the relevant date. Start at the end and work backwards. So if we took the Garlik condition of achieving 10,000 customers by the end of 2006, we would produce quarterly milestones starting with the end of the third quarter and working back through the end of the second and first quarters.

2 In regular conversations with the accountable person, take the upcoming milestone for each condition and assess the following:
   - Where are we now – what's already in place, what do we already know how to do, what's the predictable result?
   - What's the gap between the predictable result and the result we need?
   - What possible actions can we take to fill the gap?
   - What beliefs and assumptions are limiting the possible actions we can come up with? What evidence do we have for these? Can we challenge any of them and come up with more possible actions?
   - Of the possible actions, have we identified which ones will have most impact?
   - Who do we need to ask to take action and by when? Be as unreasonable as you need to be in asking for what's needed from yourself, your team and anyone else, and be very specific about what and when.

3 When a milestone has been reached for a condition, assess with the person accountable the following:
   - What's happened? What results did we get versus our expectations, and what was the gap?

- What beliefs and assumptions does this gap challenge? What have we learned? What new opportunities do we see? How should we change our approach (the means) to achieving the condition by the end of the year (the end)?
- Should we change what we seek to achieve by the next milestone without giving up on what we want to achieve by the end of the year?
- Should we change the end-of-year condition? Only do this when it's obvious it can't be met. If you are going to change it you will need to think through and deal with any consequences of a failure to meet this plan.

Towards the end of the year, when it is clear what results you are going to achieve in the plan as a whole, take stock of the results across all conditions for the entire year with your entire team:

- What's happened? What results did we get versus our expectations: what was the gap?
- What beliefs and assumptions does this gap challenge? What have you learned? Where did you fall short? What new opportunities do you see? How should you change your approach next year?
- Acknowledge and appreciate everything that was achieved and everyone's efforts.
- Re-engage everyone in what matters. Whatever happened this year, be unreasonable about the ultimate Bold and Inspiring Future goal you are committed to for your company and remind everyone of its brand promise. Produce an updated culture speech before the meeting and deliver it now.

- Agree on the targets for next year. Produce a new plan of action for the next 12 months. This plan should be designed to take the next steps towards the ultimate goal you have set yourself. These steps are informed by what you have learned in the past 12 months – you need to be clear and honest about where you are now, no fooling yourself – but not limited by what you have achieved so far. You need to stay bold and unreasonable in setting goals for the next 12 months, stretching beyond what you know how to do. (You need to hold your apparently irrational belief that ultimately you will prevail.)
- Question and discuss how you think the approaches you have used this year (the means) should be changed when implementing the new plan.

I hope you can see that two principles are being clearly demonstrated within this entire process. The first principle is a rigorous separation of ends and means. The second principle is an unreasonable commitment to the end while being totally honest and rational about what the results are telling us so we can flex the means accordingly.

Power gap principles in action

When we came to assess the results of Garlik's first year of operation at the end of 2006, it was clear that we had achieved all of our targets. We could see an interesting, profitable UK business emerging. But when we assessed the results in detail, we could see that we did not have everything in place to build our ultimate goal of a large-scale international consumer business. The results we were getting, along with everything we had learned, challenged our previous assumptions about the size of the market for the products we were offering and the costs and speed of building a large international business. It was clear we would have to change the means we were adopting to achieve the ends that we remained unreasonably committed to. Spotting this and doing something about it is a leaders' accountability.

During the brainstorm we held in order to put Garlik's 2007 plan together, CEO Tom Ilube declared that we needed to include a product that met the following ends:

- Free to consumers, at least in its most basic level.
- Easy to sign up for without compromising privacy and security. Most identity protection products, including ours, put customers through a lengthy authentication process.
- It must dramatize the whole area of digital identity such that people could understand: that digital identity exists, we all have one and it's important.
- It needed to be engaging enough to attract millions of customers without a huge marketing campaign.
- We needed to be able to launch it in 2007 in the UK and in the US soon after the UK launch.

Tom committed himself (unreasonably) to inventing and implementing such a product as one condition of our 2007 plan. Making such an unreasonable commitment instantly created a power gap for the team, which immediately saw the gap between where they were and what it would take to meet Tom's commitment. The gap focused effort on what was needed to fill it.

That's leadership in action. Leaders constantly create a very clear gap between what's needed (however unreasonable) and the current reality (however unpalatable), while keeping people's attention focused on creating ideas to fill the gap.

3. Prepare for competition

When you think you have a success on your hands, the big battles are only just starting.

Anything successful will be copied. The bigger the success, the more imitators it attracts.

This is usually only an issue that businesses need to give serious attention to in the second or third year of their life. We are just starting to focus on it now as a major issue in Garlik, about two years into the business. So I don't want to distract you too much by raising it here when your focus should be on implementing your idea – but if you don't focus on it at all, nobody else will. The leader has to worry about emerging competition and tell everyone else what to do about it.

For now I just want to give you a heads-up on what's likely to happen in the future and what you can do to prepare for it very early on.

When I think back to the businesses I've been involved in – telephone banking, mobile telephony and Internet banking in particular – and those I've observed (e.g. digital music), I've noticed that new products and services seem to go through a competitive cycle:

1   A new idea is introduced (quite often from a newcomer) and it is rapidly copied by other newcomers. (Egg was copied by Smile, Cahoot and IF; in the digital music world, Napster was copied by numerous imitators.)

2   The existing industry players dismiss all this competition as irrelevant. (As did most major banks with Egg and Internet banking. Digital music was dismissed by Sony.)

3   The initial product is often quite limited in functionality, quite expensive to produce and service, and is unprofitable – appealing only to a segment of early adopters (as was the case with the first digital music sites and digital music players).

4   The products develop rapidly until they start to appeal to a wider group of users and become cost-effective and profitable to produce. At this point, large companies who may have been previously dismissive join in the fray. (Every bank now has a major investment in Internet banking; Apple took control of digital music with the iTunes store and the iPod.)

Before I draw some conclusions from these observations, I want to refer to some academic research undertaken by Professor James Utterback (1994), formerly at Harvard Business School and now at MIT. Professor Utterback's conclusions largely support the competitive cycle I refer to, although he describes it somewhat differently. He has analysed many industries and found that a competitive cycle of some sort applies to most.

His research provides three new insights:

- The majority of innovation (new ideas implemented well) comes from newcomers.
- In about half the cases he studied, the pioneers were destroyed by competitive responses – either from large companies or other newcomers who copied the idea.
- Large companies are often ill-equipped to defend themselves from competitive attack by newcomers and this is largely an issue of culture.

This leads me to conclude that:

- Your job is far from over once the product has launched successfully. You are going to have to cycle the product through a rapid series of developments before you get it right and make it profitable. Furthermore, the more successful you are, the more competitive attacks are likely. You can't patent an idea, so even if you are able to patent aspects of your implementation (a long, expensive and difficult process), people can copy the idea and implement it in a different way.
- One way to deal with the continuous competitive threat is to create a culture where new ideas can flourish and be brought to life long after the launch of the initial product. Another solution is to create a strong, differentiated brand. Until it ran into trouble in France, Egg successfully fought off attacks from other newcomers and the world's largest banks to retain a market leadership position long after it had led the way in Internet banking. The Egg imitators (Smile, Cahoot, IF) faded back as competition escalated. This was largely due to Egg's more powerful culture and brand.
- Apple's innovative culture and cool consumer-orientated brand was key in seizing the digital music industry from the pioneers who had created it and from other large companies such as Sony, apparently better placed than Apple.

So create that brand and competitive culture, and always be alert for people who might copy your ideas.

4. Watch the cash!

For any new business, cash is king. It's important that as the leader you never forget this; in fact, you should focus on it obsessively. New businesses typically underestimate how much cash they will need, usually by overestimating sales in the early days. If you run out of cash, you go bust even if you are apparently making a profit.

Here's my advice:

- Every new company needs someone accountable for monitoring the cash – as the leader, you should talk to that person every day.
- Until you are self-funding, each plan of action needs to focus on the conditions that need to be met until the next injection of funds. Someone should be accountable for getting those new funds.
- Be conservative about cash projections – this is one area where apparent over-caution pays off in the early days.
- Conserve cash as much as possible. Spend what you have to but be as parsimonious as you can. This can be very hard if you have been used to the free spending that is common in big businesses.

In terms of business economics, you should worry about things in this order:

- Having or generating enough cash to keep going.
- Building long-term value. This is created when you achieve something now that has the possibility of creating a profitable cash flow sometime in the future. Signing up millions of customers for a free product, such as Facebook, creates no immediate profitable cash flow but creates value in the expectation that in the future you will

be able to sell something to those customers or to those who wish to advertise to them. Valuation techniques for new businesses try to measure the long-term value that is being created.

- Product profitability: You have to have a reasonable expectation that each product you sell will at some time in the future be profitable. It may not be so in the early days because product costs may be higher than product revenues until you achieve sufficient scale economics in product sales and operation or because initially you have to discount heavily to get a foothold in the market.

- Company profitability. This occurs when product profitability exceeds the costs of growing the business plus overheads. Profit only comes when a critical mass of customers and product sales is achieved. Even when you achieve critical mass, it often makes sense to grow the business faster, assuming you have enough cash and give priority to building long-term value rather than worry about short-term profit. Making this trade-off is one reason why private equity comprehensively outperforms public markets.

- Going public. All of the above apply to private companies, including venture capital and private equity-funded companies. Once you go public, the rules change and short-term profit becomes king – which would be a nice problem to have.

5. Take risks with care

Leadership involves a constant series of choices about what to do, what not to do and when to do it. For example:

- What new products do we invest in this year?
- What suppliers do we choose to work with?
- Where should we focus our marketing efforts this year?

- How much money should we invest in marketing this year?
- How much should we invest in expanding our production?

Any choice that involves a relatively large investment and has relatively unpredictable results represents a risk for the business. You will have to take risks, but they should all be taken consciously and after proper consideration. This is an important subject and is covered in depth in Chapter 10.

6. Create a hot leadership team

In many ways, creating and maintaining a hot leadership team is the most important thing you will need to do. By 'hot' I mean committed to a common goal, along with the talent and determination to succeed no matter what happens to set you back or throw you off course. This topic gets the whole of Chapter 11 to itself, but for now just consider what two leaders I spoke to recently advised me about this subject.

Peter Darbee and his team are committed to putting in the practices of a high-performance team; they are working with Gordon Starr on further developing their power as a hot team using many of the principles I describe in Chapter 11.

'One of my objectives is to attract the best people in the world to PG&E. The leadership team is vital.

'None of us really need to work but we love coming here. We think what we are doing is very important. We have a charter for our leadership team:

'In support of our vision we pledge to each other our integrity, our unwavering stand for one another's success and our legacy as leaders.'

Peter Darbee, Chairman, PG&E

'I believe you only get things done through great teams. The three of us (the founders) have complimentary skills and we have now built a management team of eight people. We recruit carefully, finding talented people whose values resonate with ours, who take work seriously but not themselves too seriously and who are committed rational altruists. We invest time in relationships and making the team work well.'

Richard Reed, co-founder, Innocent Drinks

The leadership list

I recommend that the first thing you do when you set up a business is copy the following list, which summarizes my six accountabilities of leadership for entrepreneurs. Keep it with you and look at it every day. Ask yourself each day: how am I doing on these issues, what new things should I start doing, what should I do more of and what should I stop doing? You may want to talk to a trusted member of your team or a mentor or coach to get some feedback from time to time.

- Regularly recreate an empowering culture.
- Maintain the 'power gap'.
- Prepare for competition.
- Watch the cash.
- Choose the risks you take with care.
- Create and maintain a hot leadership team.

Do something

Undertake the following exercise based on the power gap approach I have described. You can do this alone or with others. Start with the draft action plan you produced in Chapter 6.

Pick one condition of satisfaction.

Imagine the business was starting tomorrow. Come up with the first milestone for that condition: produce a statement of what you will have achieved in the first three months of the business on the way to satisfying the condition at the end of 12 months.

For this milestone, assess the following:

- What's already in place? What do we already know how to do? What would be the predictable result?
- What would be the gap between the predictable result and the result we need?
- What possible actions could we take immediately to fill the gap?
- What are the beliefs and assumptions that are limiting the possible actions we can come up with?
- What evidence do we have for these? Can we challenge any of them and come up with more possible actions?
- Of the possible actions, have we identified which ones will have most impact?
- Which actions would we take now if this were for real?
- What would be the first thing we would do and by when?

When you are building a business for real, you will find yourself constantly assessing where you are against the next milestone on each condition and constantly focusing people on the gap between what's predictable and what's needed. You will be urging people into action to fill the gap – that's just a reflection of the central principles of leadership:

- Be totally realistic about where you are now and what results you will get if you carry on doing what you are doing.
- Be unreasonable in your belief and determination to succeed in the long term.
- Focus people on the gap between what's currently predictable and what you actually need to achieve in the short term.
- Demand action from people to fill the gap between what's predictable and what's needed.

Answers to my seminar questions on leadership

When seminar participants are asked the questions I previously posed to you about leadership, they always conclude that leadership is essentially about making change happen. As the discussion continues, they usually come close to a dictionary definition of leader: *A leader is someone who shows others the way (by going first).*

10

The smart risks principle

'Life is a sum of all your choices.'

Albert Camus

Life constantly presents us with a succession of choices, all of which carry potential risks and rewards. Some have little consequence ('Cappuccino or latte?'); others can be life-changing in a way that is completely unknown at the time ('Do I accept that dinner invitation?'). The third category is perhaps the most interesting. It involves choices where some assessment of the likely consequence is possible, such as 'Do I take this new job?', 'Do we move house?' or 'Do I marry that person?'

Choosing what risks to take and avoid is a key skill that every successful entrepreneur needs to develop. This fact was put to me most eloquently by Terry Rhodes, Chief Strategy Officer of $3bn mobile phone company Celtel. He now lectures on entrepreneurism at the London Business School.

'Successful entrepreneurs don't take big, unconsidered risks and they don't do great leaps of faith – they approach their Bold and Inspiring Future goals with a series of considered decisions.'

This very same thought has echoed in countless conversations I have had with entrepreneurs recently. I call it the *smart risks principle*: each big decision you take along the route should be carefully assessed so that any risks are approached both consciously and intelligently. This smart risks principle helps you make big decisions wisely.

A big decision has one or more of the following characteristics:

- It is not easily and simply reversed.
- It commits a significant amount of time and/or effort.
- It puts a significant amount of money at risk.

When you are implementing a new idea or creating a new business, you are presented with a succession of big decisions. The biggest decisions you have taken so far are the ones you implicitly took when you put together your plan of action for the first 12 months in Chapter 6. These included what markets to address, what technology to use, what products to develop, what people to employ and where to spend money. Every year when you put a new action plan together you will be faced with similar decisions – 'How do I use the resources I have available to take the next step forward?'

Two sorts of decision

In the early years of a new business, you are usually faced with two sorts of decision:

- Big unavoidable choices. These are decisions where a choice of some sort must be made, e.g. if you need a computer system, you have to select the most appropriate one.

- Optional avoidable choices. These are decisions you could potentially avoid, e.g. whether to buy another business that has become available, whether to expand into another country or whether to develop and launch a new product.

Unavoidable choices

I will always remember the first unavoidable choice I had to make at Firstdirect. It concerned the computer system required to run the current accounts at the heart of Firstdirect's family of products. We had three possibilities:

1   Buy a new system that had all the flexibility we needed but had a high implementation risk.
2   Use a system that had just been developed to run the small portfolio of sterling current accounts maintained by Midland Bank's international division. This option had less flexibility than buying a new system but less implementation risk.
3   Use the same system that Midland branches used to run the millions of current accounts they maintained. This had a low implementation risk but lacked flexibility. With this option we also risked getting stuck in the development backlog that all banks experience with their key systems.

Once we had made this choice we would be stuck with it. We would invest a lot of money and time in the chosen system, and it would not be possible to launch on time and stay within budget if we had to reverse our decision. It was a tough call. The Firstdirect chairman was urging me to go one way, the Firstdirect IT expert another and the Midland Bank CIO yet another.

Once again it helped when I remembered that this was *my* soap opera; I got to decide what choices to take and how my script unfurled. I urged myself to choose wisely: as the script-writer and leading actor, you certainly don't get to blame anyone else if it all goes wrong.

In this case I chose the third option, the system that the Midland Bank branches used. It turned out to be a very smart choice – I'll tell you how I made it later.

Optional investments

At Egg I was constantly faced with choices about optional investments. There was so much opportunity in those crazy dot com years. Here are three big investments I chose to recommend to the Board and that we went on to take:

- Development of a credit card – the Egg card.
- Development of an investment supermarket.
- A joint credit/loyalty card with Boots.

… and here are three opportunities I considered but didn't pursue:

- A major play in digital banking via interactive TV or mobile phones (we did small pilots in each).
- Purchase of a mortgage supermarket that had grown impressively since its IPO a year previously.
- Purchase of a US Internet bank.

Of the investments we chose to make, the Egg card was a spectacular success and was indeed critical to Egg's future profit stream and value, something that wasn't obvious when I made

the decision. The investment supermarket and the joint cards with Boots were not spectacular successes but were not disasters either.

Events proved that we were wise to avoid the three investments I passed on.

How to take smart risks

If you are faced with a big decision, whether it's an unavoidable choice or an optional investment, you should consider the following questions before making your final decision:

- Are we crystal clear about what we are taking on if we go this way: what problems we will have to solve, what investment of time and reputation are involved, and what compromises we are going to have to make in other areas of the business?
- Is the potential upside worth the personal and financial investment?
- Would we back ourselves to pull this off more than five times out of ten, even if the circumstances (economic and competitive conditions) we meet are a good deal less favourable than we are assuming?
- What would we have to believe to think this would be successful – do we believe that?
- Can we afford to fail at this without fatally damaging our ambitions – either because we can't afford the write off or because it would leave our reputation in tatters?

If you can answer 'yes' to all of those questions, it is a smart risk indeed – something that Virgin has turned into an art form over the years.

'Don't take risks on the basis of fear of failure. Manage risks to minimize failure. We need to take risks; everything in life is a risk. When Richard Branson started Virgin Atlantic, he realized he had to protect the downside. He struck a deal with Boeing to lease the plane. If it hadn't have worked out, he could have given it back.'

Will Whitehorn, President, Virgin Galactica

––––––––––

'In the case of the airline, I had worked out exactly how much I was risking and it was less than a third of one year's profit from the music business. It wasn't much of a gamble but I thought running an airline would be fun, and the potential outcome was worth it.'

Richard Branson, 1998

––––––––––

Do something

Make a list of four or five big decisions you have taken in the past either at home or at work. Apply the smart risk criteria:

- How did you feel about these decisions when you took them?
- How smart were these decisions based on the smart risk criteria?
- How did they work out in practice?
- Are there any lessons for you out of how you took these decisions and what happened?

This exercise will give you an immediate appreciation of the way the smart risks principle works and how you to use it when faced with any key decisions.

It was considering the smart risk questions that led me to choose the Midland Bank branch system for Firstdirect:

- I was much clearer about what I would be taking on with that choice than with the alternatives; I knew what compromises I would have to make to product features and I could live with them.
- It was the lowest cost alternative both financially and personally. The potential upsides of the other solutions (more flexibility, real-time updates) were not worth the extra risks.
- I backed us to pull off all of the available choices five times out of ten but this option was significantly less risky.
- I had to believe I could get priority resource allocation for some amendments we needed to make to the system to make Firstdirect work – this was a risk given the IT development backlog but I had reasonable reasons to believe it would happen.
- It would be hard to fail at this and keep on track but that was true of any choice I could make.

When I considered the three optional investments we made at Egg, I could answer all five questions positively:

- We had sufficient understanding and expertise of the areas we were going into.
- The potential returns were definitely worth the investment.
- We could be reasonably confident of our ability to implement the products.
- The assumptions we made about the likely financial outcome were reasonable.
- We could afford to fail without running out of money.

I found I could barely answer one question positively about the investments we didn't make at Egg and yet, intuitively, neither I nor my team had initially dismissed these investments out of hand.

This approach to assessing big decisions is deceptively powerful – don't let its apparent simplicity fool you.

'Bet the company' decisions

Sometimes you are faced with a choice where you can't afford to make the wrong decision. This happens when you have to make a decision that gets a 'yes' to the first four questions of the smart risk assessment approach but gets a 'no' to the fifth one. I call this a *'bet the company' decision*.

Choosing to launch the Egg credit card turned out to be a 'bet the company' decision in that it was the product that made all the money. If it had failed, Egg would have failed – but I didn't know that at the time I made the decision. So that wasn't a particularly brave decision, although it was a very smart one.

The brave 'bet the company' decisions are those that are optional investment choices where it is clear you cannot afford to fail at the time you take them. These are quite rare. Entrepreneurs don't bet the company too often!

I can only remember taking one such decision. In April 1999 I decided, with the Board's support, to switch Egg from a telephone operation supported by the Internet to an Internet operation supported by the telephone. From that day, all new accounts would have to be opened via the Internet and we would put all of our development efforts into Internet products and services.

At the time I took the decision, we were continuing to acquire new customers through the telephone at a record rate. We needed to slow things down for a while, but we were coping and there were many ways to ease demand for a while without taking too many risks with the business.

Switching to the Internet certainly slowed demand for a while. But it was primarily a big strategic bet that enough people would be prepared to apply for financial products and service them online, and that in an online world there would be many more profitable products and services we could provide to customers than through the telephone. Egg had always intended to switch to the Internet, but this was three years ahead of plan and at a time when most big banks around the world were dismissing the Internet as irrelevant. We took this risk to get ahead of the game, set the agenda for banking and create an online future.

We assessed our move to the Internet carefully. The whole management team visited the US to talk to the Internet giants of the time (Sun, Cisco, Microsoft, Oracle, Lycos and eBay) and to be clear on the scope of the opportunity and what it would take to pull it off.

It was a smart risk in every way except that we could not afford to fail. Our reputation would have been fatally damaged and we would have probably run out of cash (and Prudential's willingness to invest) before we could rebuild a telephone business. However, the potential upside made it a risk worth taking as far as I was concerned.

Our decision provoked huge controversy, making the front page of the *FT* and getting a huge amount of air time on radio and TV. Throughout the day that our big move was announced, I was attacked by almost everybody – 'You must be out of your mind' from the business press and 'It's not fair to exclude people who don't have an Internet connection' from the consumer press.

Then at the end of the day, Goldman Sachs published a note applauding the move and naming Egg as one of the most attractive Internet investment opportunities in the world. The Prudential share price soared (Egg was 100%-owned by Prudential at the time) and Egg.com was born. Egg never looked back until a fateful decision to invest in France in 2002.

When Apple launched the Macintosh in 1984, they ran a massive marketing campaign initiated by a stunning and iconic ad shown during the Super Bowl. Directed by Ridley Scott, it showed a female athlete wearing a white top with a picture of Apple's Macintosh computer on it, running through a nightmare totalitarian world to throw a sledgehammer at a TV image of Big Brother, believed to represent Apple's then great rival IBM. As I saw it, the ad was saying that only Apple could save the world from a horrible centralist future. Apple empowered the individual.

Apple's Chairman John Scully later described the launch of the Mac as a 'bet the company' decision. Given Apple's financial and market position at the time and the amount of money they had invested in the development, he was probably right. The ad itself was also close to a 'bet the company' decision – it was highly controversial and it could have easily ruined Apple's reputation.

Luckily for them, it became one of the most successful ads of all time. It was a powerful talking point watched by a huge audience. Their big 'bet the company' decision had come off at a level of pure genius. The ad created such a media frenzy that it gained many subsequent free TV airings and print mentions as it was discussed in the media. At the time, Nielsen ratings estimated that the commercial reached 46.4% of American households (50% of all men and 36% of women).

Advertising Age magazine named it the 1980s' 'Commercial of the Decade' and in 1999, the *TV Guide* magazine in the US selected it as number one in their list of '50 Greatest Commercials of All Time'. (*TV Guide* also listed the commercial as number 93 on their list of 'The Best Moments in TV History' – the only commercial on the list.)

The lesson I would draw from all of this is that there will be times where you are going to face the prospect of a 'bet the company' decision either because there are no choices that don't put everything at risk or because the potential upside of such a decision becomes irresistible. In such cases, do at least make sure the first four criteria of a smart risk are taken care of and good luck.

Not-so-smart risks

There will be times when what seemed like a smart risk turns out to be not so smart after all – that's just business for you. If this happens you just have to learn what you can from it, draw on your natural resilience, write your next chapter and move on.

If a risk goes wrong, even if it was a 'bet the company' risk, it doesn't mean that:

- You were stupid to take it.
- You should be more careful next time. Over-caution is a common reaction to a smart risk that goes wrong and it normally makes everything worse. You get nowhere without taking risks.
- You will never be successful. Almost all success stories have failures and recovery from apparently impossible odds. Resilience and a 'never say die' attitude are what distinguishes winners.

I had retired as CEO and was part-time Vice Chairman when Egg took a decision to launch a business in France. What we all thought was a smart risk turned out not to be for reasons that were somewhat unpredictable at the time.

In 2002, we announced that Egg was investing £100m in France, an amount it could easily afford to lose in accordance with the smart risk criteria. Even though the total closure costs were much higher than that, the total investment remained within Egg's ability to fund without getting into trouble.

Here's what went wrong according to reports in *The Daily Telegraph* (I prefer to use public domain sources in telling this story to avoid breaching any confidences):

- In April 2003, Egg CEO Paul Gratton described the launch as 'botched'.
- A botched launch meant the costs of recovering and building a sustainable business escalated to the point where Egg could not afford to take them alone.
- Egg sought a deal with another bank to share the costs and build a business together in France. This turned into a public auction by Prudential for the 80% of Egg shares that it then owned. This dragged on for a year and did not end successfully.
- The combination of being for sale and trying to deal with the problems in France stretched the management to breaking point and beyond, diverting attention from the key issues facing the UK business as the credit climate deteriorated in the UK.
- The cost of getting out of France escalated while the auction process ran on.

Egg was widely criticized for not realizing how difficult it would be to build a business in France. In fact, more than one expert has said to me recently that 'Egg must have been out of its mind to go into France'. We'd heard that from experts before but this time they were right. However, I remain convinced that Egg saw an opportunity in France that other people couldn't and, with a bit more luck and better execution, it may well have paid off.

The unpredictable event was the botched launch (something you wouldn't have expected given the quality of our team) and then the failed auction. According to the *Telegraph*, Prudential spurned at least one opportunity to sell at a reasonable price. Prudential eventually purchased the 20% of shares in Egg that it didn't own and tried to integrate Egg. I'd left by then, but I didn't give that particular strategy any chance of success at all.

A much diminished Egg, with all of its key management having jumped ship, was eventually sold to Citibank in 2007 at what must have been a very disappointing price for Prudential. I hope Egg will re-emerge as a powerful and radical brand, but all of the major players in the drama have moved on. Many ex-Egg employees are demonstrating great leadership and success in new roles; some have gone on to create new businesses. That's just soap opera for you.

Do something

Go back to the draft action plan that you produced in Chapter 6 and make a list of the big decisions implicit within it. Remember that a big decision has one or more of the following characteristics:

- It is not easily and simply reversed once made.
- It commits a significant amount of time and/or effort.
- It puts a significant amount of money at risk.

Separate the big decisions into unavoidable choices and optional investments. An unavoidable choice is a decision you have to make; an optional investment involves an elective opportunity or investment that has risks and rewards associated with it.

Pick two or three big decisions and apply the smart risks principle. Do they feel like smart risks? If not, could you amend the decision in some way to make it a smart risk?

Doing this will give you some much-needed practice in considering choices using the smart risks principle and help you avoid making some big mistakes in the future.

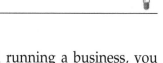

When you are actually creating and running a business, you should use the smart risks principle to assess each big decision. The general rule is to only take smart risks unless it is one of those unavoidable 'bet the company' decisions where you can't afford to fail. In that case, make sure you have:

- assessed the risk carefully
- made the choice that is most likely to succeed
- given a lot of personal attention to managing the risk throughout its implementation.

11

Hot teams

'Never doubt that a small group of thoughtful, committed people can change the world. Indeed, it is the only thing that ever has.'

Margaret Mead, anthropologist

However driven, talented or enthusiastic you are, it is highly unlikely that you will be able to build a successful company all on your own. Successful companies are built by a strong leader who engages a powerful leadership team, fires them up and keeps them hot. Creating and maintaining that group of thoughtful and committed people is one of the most important things that you must do on the way to your Bold and Inspiring Future. In fact, almost everything you have done to date has not only got your company started but has also helped to create all the necessary conditions needed to establish your powerful leadership team.

The team versus the individual

'Personal leadership is one of the most studied topics in American life. Indeed, I have devoted a big chunk of my professional life to better understanding its workings. Far less studied – and perhaps more important – is group leadership. The disparity of interest in those two realms of leadership is logical, given the strong individualist bent of American culture. But the more I look at the history of business, government, the arts and the sciences, the clearer it is that few great accomplishments are ever the work of a single individual.'

Warren Bennis, 1997

When it comes to deciding whether to part with their hard-earned cash, investors will no doubt concern themselves with the power of your team too. Indeed, the two most prestigious investors in Silicon Valley, Kleiner Perkins and Sequoia Capital, made an early $25m investment in Google in 1999 based on the impressive partnership between the founders Sergey Brin and Larry Page.

According to David Vise, whose meticulously researched book *The Google Story* chronicles the company's development, Sequoia's Michael Moritz had seen over and over again how start-up companies founded by pairs of entrepreneurs that shared a common vision had a greater chance of success than lone individuals.

Bill Gates and Paul Allen, the co-founders of Microsoft, spring to mind, as do Steve Jobs and Steve Wozniak, who started Apple. In both these cases, a small leadership team quickly coalesced around the founders.

The power of the team in getting investment was also demonstrated to me at Garlik. Nigel Grierson of Doughy Hanson told me as we negotiated the deal that they would only invest if he was sure that both Tom Ilube and myself were committed – they were not investing in either of us individually but in the two of us. They were just as concerned to judge the quality of the rest of the leadership team. We therefore chose three other team members who were as committed to Garlik as Tom and I were to pitch to them. It was enough of a team to secure funding.

You can of course also find funding if you are a sole founder. But what is absolutely true is that you are unlikely to be successful unless you create a small, committed leadership team to work with you. This can be anything up to ten people, but in the early days it's more likely to be between three and five.

What is a hot team?

'None of us is as smart as all of us. That's good, because the problems we face are too complex to be solved by any one person or any one discipline. Our only chance is to bring people together from a variety of backgrounds and disciplines who can refract a problem through the prism of complementary minds allied in common purpose. I call such collections of talent Great Groups. The genius of Great Groups is that they get remarkable people – strong individual achievers – to work together to get results. But these groups serve a second and equally important function: they provide psychic support and personal fellowship. They help generate courage. Without a sounding board for outrageous ideas, without personal encouragement and perspective when we hit a roadblock, we'd all lose our way.'

Warren Bennis, 1997

The essential characteristics of a hot team are to provide psychic support and personal fellowship, and to get breakthrough results doing what they love. Essentially, a hot team makes you happy to be at work. I have therefore made it a personal priority to create a hot leadership team wherever I have worked.

Hot teams are obvious

If I wander into any company that has retained a level of dynamism as it has grown (e.g. Mother, Ideo and Apple), I expect to notice how noisy and lively it all feels. There will be ad hoc conversations going on everywhere; the energy will feel palpable. Peering into meeting rooms, I will notice how wild it all looks. People will be on their feet, drawing on the walls (hopefully having put some paper up first). The debates will be fast and furious; people will often burst into laughter. I instinctively know that at the heart of that sort of organization is a hot team.

In contrast, when I wander into the offices of most large corporations these days, I usually notice three things:

1. A deadening atmosphere.
2. Ranks of people sitting in cathedral-like-quiet, (apparently) working diligently on PCs – probably devoting time to Facebook.
3. Meeting rooms full of people sitting around tables with little sign of life in them.

If you don't create and maintain a hot leadership team, that's exactly where you are headed. You'll get there surprisingly quickly, often within a year or two from the start of your company. Large corporations can afford to be deadening places to work: they have assets, scale and huge financial muscle, but a hot leadership team is the key to creating and maintaining the culture that keeps young businesses alive. Right now all you have is your talent and commitment – you can't afford to let your fire go out.

Do something

At this point it's a good idea to get a sense of what it might be like to actually build and lead a hot team.

So think of a team you admire or have admired in the past. It could have been a team you were part of, a team you have watched in action or a business team or a sports team, or indeed any team that worked or played together with a common purpose:

- What made the team hot?
- What did you most admire about it?
- Who created the team?

What would it feel like to create and lead a team like that?

Creating and maintaining a hot team

'I believe, behind every great leader is a great group, an effective partnership. And making up every Great Group is a unique construct of strong, often eccentric individuals. So the question for organizations is; how do you get talented, self-absorbed, often arrogant, incredibly bright people to work together?'

Warren Bennis, 1997

For most organizations, that really is a hard question. Luckily, it shouldn't be so hard for you: if you have followed the steps I have described so far, you will have the beginnings of a hot team already. You should have already infected people with your own enthusiasm, carefully recruited an initial team and together generated product ideas and pitched for funding to create your Bold and Inspiring Future. People who share a vision that they are all committed to start off hot. Your job is to keep them hot and make them hotter every day. What you want is for people to look at your team and say: 'Wow, those guys are on fire!'

Sadly, keeping the team hot is not as easy as firing them up in the first place. Our initial commitment and passion starts to fade when we confront the problems of creating a new business. We cool down as we confront the harsh realities of the moment (as we must, to stay on the edge of reason). Although we get a bit warmer every time we realign ourselves towards our Bold and Inspiring Future, that's not enough. Hot teams thrive when the leader maintains a powerful context and develops team practices that keep velocity, energy and spirits high and relationships strong.

Staying hot – context is decisive

'Context is the human environment that determines the limitations of your actions and the scope of results your actions can produce.'

Tracy Goss, 1996

Context provides the meaning that we assign to events and the conclusions we draw as a result of those meanings. It is your job to influence the context of your leadership team in every conversation that you have with them about any significant event.

People construct their own meanings about things that happen. If, for example, you lose business from a client, that means: *Our product wasn't good enough.* And every meaning leads to a conclusion: *We must invest more in product development.*

Of course, different people are likely to assign a different meaning and draw different conclusions from the same event: other people may conclude that you lost the business because:

- the salesperson didn't sell the product well enough, which means you need a new sales approach
- you got the pricing wrong, which means you need to cut your costs so that you can cut your prices.
- your quality wasn't good enough, which means you need more support staff.

In general, where there is some doubt, people will tend to choose negative meanings and draw gloomy conclusions – that just seems to be a default of human nature.

Left unchecked, this natural human tendency to draw different (but often negative) conclusions from the same event can lead to endless arguments about what each event means and what should be done about it. This soon becomes a blame game where team members decide whose fault it is and the internal battles begin. This causes a team to cool very quickly, irrelevant of whether such arguments are held in the open or whether the leader suppresses them and they explode in the corridors.

So you need to help the team to come to a shared understanding of what each significant event and incident in a company's life means, and what you are going to do about it. Transformational leadership expert Tracy Goss has designed a process for doing this that I have used consistently since she first described it to me in 1997:

1   Focus the team's attention on what happened – just the facts, not what it all means. It's generally both easy and incredibly valuable to get agreement to just the facts, e.g. 'We made a bid to provide company X with product Y at price Z. They declined our offer and chose our competitor instead.'

2   Engage the team in a simple question: 'What's missing that would make a difference?' In the example that I have been using, the question would be 'What's missing from our offer that would make a difference?' It's surprising how often that simple question gets rapid alignment, whereas an apparently similar question, 'What's wrong with our offer?', leads to endless argument

3   Ask your team 'What's next and what actions shall we take to move forward from here?'

You can use this simple structure in every conversation you have with your leadership team about what's happened – in formal or informal meetings, or one-to-one. It's deceptively simple but, used consistently, it will make a big difference. It creates a context of: 'There's nothing wrong and no one to blame – how can we move forward from here?' That's a great way to keep focused and maintain velocity.

Practices of a hot team

The following practices are additional things you can and should do on a regular basis in order to keep your team hot:

- Create an enemy outside the company.
- Involve the whole team in major decisions but don't seek consensus.
- Hold regular progress meetings.

- Get the whole team engaged in giving feedback in design reviews.
- Use breakdown meetings to solve problems.
- Brainstorming.
- Give time to relationship meetings.
- Use one-to-one meetings for a little light coaching.

Create an enemy outside the company

> '*An enemy raises the stakes of the competition, it helps your group rally and define itself (as everything the enemy is not), and it also frees you to be spurred by that time-honoured motivator, self-righteous hatred. Research by social psychologists confirms that competition with an outsider boosts creativity, whereas win-lose competition within a team diminishes it.*'

Warren Bennis, 1997

From the start of the dot com boom in 1998 until quite recently, it seemed like every new software start-up had the so called evil empire of Microsoft as its enemy. Apple focused on IBM, which it characterized as Big Brother. Google (with its 'do no evil' motto) focused on all traditional big corporations. Mercury hated BT, Virgin Atlantic hated BA. Egg's enemy were all of the traditional banks who (Egg claimed) took advantage of people's lack of financial sophistication to rip them off. Egg tended to focus on Barclays – not because they were any worse than the others, but mainly because they were the biggest credit card competitors.

Having an enemy to defeat, particularly one you can genuinely hate, provides a lot of energy to a team. It's normally quite easy to define an enemy: Ask yourself which big company in your industry is almost the opposite of you in their values and beliefs or represents the biggest threat. Which big company would you most like to do battle with and destroy?

Involve the whole team in major decisions but don't seek consensus

Get the team together to make decisions or deal with issues where you genuinely open to various possibilities – so obviously you can't have already made up your mind. You need to be clear about who is accountable for making each decision. Allow all participants to have their say, but have the person accountable decide on the subsequent course of action.

This approach stops two things that can cool a team down:

1   Trying to get everyone to buy into every big decision – the consensus trap that kills velocity and reduces energy.
2   People feeling they have no voice in major decisions, which depresses the team spirit.

'Consensus is neither useful nor necessary. It slows everything down for no purpose. The way to maintain power is to let the accountable person take the decision with no compromise, but before that decision is taken let everybody have their say. They will at least have the experience of being heard and what they say can be useful input for the person actually making the decision.'

Tracy Goss, speaking to the Egg leadership team, 2000

Hold regular progress meetings

A progress meeting assesses your advances towards the next deadline in your action plan. The meeting should be short (no more than an hour) and focus on action. It's a great way to keep the power gap very much in people's minds for the next milestone that they are accountable for.

The key thing about these meetings is that they are used to maintain velocity. Velocity is killed by endless hours spent creating and debating explanations, and making excuses when results get behind plan. You don't want that. You want people to stay in action by asking themselves: 'Where am I now?', 'What's the gap to the next milestone?', 'What am I going to do by next week to start to fill that gap?'

Get the whole team engaged in giving feedback in design reviews

Design reviews are aimed at getting some feedback and suggestions to a planned design (a product, a website, a marketing or PR campaign, a strategy or a budget) at an intermediate point in the design process. These meetings are a great way to reinforce what the company and its brand stand for; they keep everyone involved in the sexiest part of the business and, as a consequence, keep energy and spirits high.

Use breakdown meetings to solve problems

Breakdowns occur when an apparently insoluble problem is preventing progress or where it seems as though an important result is now impossible. Unresolved and unacknowledged breakdowns kill everything that makes a team hot: they kill velocity, depress team spirit, diminish energy and can destroy relationships if people start to point fingers at each other.

The first thing about breakdowns is to acknowledge the problem as soon as it becomes apparent. Don't try and deny it exists, and don't try and apply a quick fix – accept that you don't know how to fix it at the moment. Just acknowledging that the problem exists calms everyone down.

The next step is to get the team together for a breakdown meeting:

1   Start the meeting by talking about the breakdown in as relaxed a way as you can. Tell everyone the facts and admit that you don't know how to solve the problem. Don't let anyone try and propose a quick fix. Here are a few questions you might pose:
    –   What exactly has happened/is happening? Stick to the facts – don't allow opinions, justifications or excuses to come in at this point.
    –   Why is this a problem?
    –   Is it really worth solving or should we just let it go?
2   Once you can express the problem clearly and succinctly, and once you are clear that it is a problem worth solving, try and get to the source of it. Ask everyone:
    –   Why did this problem show up? Having heard everyone, state your conclusion and see if this can be verified in some way.
    –   Why did this situation occur? Again, listen to everyone, come to a conclusion and try to verify it in some way.
    –   Repeat until you get an 'Ah ha!' moment, i.e. you feel you have got to the source of the problem.

A simple hypothetical example might be useful:

> Q   Why aren't we getting as much traffic as we need to our website from all that press coverage?
>
> A   The stories don't really contain a call to action.
>
> Q   Why don't the stories contain a call to action?
>
> A   We give too much information in the press release – there is nothing more for people to do.
>
> Q   Why do we give too much information in the press release?
>
> A   Because we are trying to be bullet-proof in what we say, so we pack our stories with facts and supporting evidence and academic-like argument.
>
> Q   Why do we need to be bullet-proof?
>
> A   Because we don't want to be controversial.
>
> Q   Why don't we want to be controversial?
>
> A   Because we weren't too sure of our ground when we launched and we didn't want to be immediately attacked by experts who disagreed with us.
>
> Ah ha! When we launched, we didn't want to be attacked by experts. That's no longer an issue, but we are still behaving as though it is and that's the source of this particular problem – a fear of being controversial. Maybe we are surer of our ground now or less vulnerable to attack. Or maybe we have to give up the fear of being controversial in order to move on.

So now you have the problem and its source defined, you will need to find the solution one step at a time.

- What could we do to solve the problem? Brainstorm solutions, write them down and cluster them into similar ideas.
- Pick the ten biggest ideas.

- Take each big idea and assess it in terms of how likely it is to solve the problem with the time and resources you have.
- Decide which ideas you will go for. (Often there is more than one.)
- List agreed actions, decide who is accountable and by when.

Brainstorming

> *'Everybody thinks they know what brainstorming is. They don't. Brainstorming can be a skill or an art. You can become a brainstorming virtuoso, deliver more value, create more energy, foster more innovation through better brainstorming.'*

Tom Kelley, 1995

All hot teams are exceptionally good at creating new ideas. New ideas are the lifeblood of a hot team – they keep velocity, spirits and energy high. A brainstorm meeting should positively fizz with energy.

Imagine being in an ordinary company competing against a hot team in another company. It feels like you are in the middle of a whirlwind, with new product and marketing ideas flying at you, giving you no time to think or respond. At its best, Egg attempted, with some success, to create that feeling in other banks.

Creating a brainstorming competence in your team is the way to achieve this. Brainstorming allows you to suspend judgment and change your normal way of looking at things in order to generate creative ideas that didn't exist before the group converged.

The key principles:

- All you need is a room, notepads, pens, Post-it notes and flip charts, or something similar.
- The meeting should last no more than two hours.
- People should be well briefed with any background information and you should set the meeting up with a clear briefing on what's needed. For example, we want ideas for a new product that:
  - will get at least 100,000 sales this year
  - will make at least £5 profit per sale
  - can be sold to existing customers whenever we have an opportunity to communicate with them
  - will cost less than £250,000 to develop
  - can be launched within three months.
- Keep the meeting focused on that topic.
- Encourage wild ideas and ask people to build on the ideas of others.
- Only allow one person to talk at any one time.
- As ideas emerge, write them down on flip charts and number them. Don't let anyone assess an idea at this stage, but do let people ask questions about the idea and encourage them to build on it.
- Go through the ideas and cluster them into groups of similar ideas, labelling each cluster with a descriptive title. You will find the individual ideas will cluster into a small number of big ideas with a few outliers, which you can discard.
- Pick the three clusters that you think have the highest likelihood of success. Work up a quick assessment of what it will take to make these happen. Pick a winner. Produce an action plan charting who is going to do what by when.

'The Space remembers: cover virtually every wall and flat sur-
face with paper before the session begins. That way, you won't
find yourself in the awkward situation of having to erase ideas
to make room for more. And you may find there's a certain syn-
ergy in moving around the room writing down and sketching
ideas. When you return to a spot on the wall where an idea was
captured, spatial memory will help people recapture the mindset
they had when the idea first emerged.'

Tom Kelley, 1995

Give time to relationship meetings

Hot teams thrive on relationships. These relationships need to be
based on trust, respect, admiration and appreciation. It's a sad
fact of life that unless we focus on these qualities in others, we
don't really see them. Instead we focus on our opinions of what's
right about someone or what's wrong with them.

Regular team relationship meetings are invaluable in helping
to keep individual relationships strong. These meetings should
be held in relaxed surroundings and attendees should be encouraged to get to know each other as individuals. These meetings
are often best lubricated with a little food and wine – but not too
much, for obvious reasons. The idea is to create an environment
that feels relaxed, warm and supportive – not anarchical.

In the meeting:

- Let everyone say what they have achieved in the last
  three months and what they feel good about. Ask others
  to acknowledge and appreciate what they have done.
- Reinforce your priorities and strategy. Make sure everyone is clear about what's important right now, why it's
  important and what you are relying on them to achieve.

- Let people say what's bothering them, acknowledge where they are struggling and ask for help. Assistance is always forthcoming in successful meetings where people get behind each other.

Gordon Starr used to say to me that 'relationship is the foundation of accomplishment'. He often ran little exercises like this when a team first formed or when a new member joined:

'Have each member share something personal with the team – what they do professionally, something about their family, or something about a passion in life. Next, ask each person to share what he or she can be counted on to bring to the team.

'Have the rest of the team enhance whatever the speaker says they will bring to the team (e.g. "In addition to what you just said, you bring humour and lightness") in such a way that the speaker sits down feeling fully validated, having discovered ways in which they contribute that they were not previously aware of. Even if you have only just met them, you will be able to distinguish things to validate simply by listening to the information they have shared with you.

'The person receiving the enhancement: your job is simply to say thank you. Take your team's communication as a gift. Don't deflect it.'

Gordon Starr, Starr Consulting Group Inc.

Use one-to-one meetings for a little light coaching

Some straightforward coaching is very helpful in reinforcing hot team characteristics in one-to-one meetings where the person is telling you of some rather ill-defined concern. You want to help them to be clear on what's really bothering them and what can be done about it immediately.

There is a really easy process for this. Just ask the following questions and listen carefully to the reply. You don't have to memorize the list; you can read it out one question at a time and then give them all your attention as they respond and reflect each of their answers back to them until they agree that's exactly what they meant.

1   Tell me about something that's really bothering you at the moment.
2   How do you feel about it – what bothers you most about it and what's its impact on you, particularly on your energy and vitality?
3   What outcome are you seeking to this issue?
4   What will achieving that outcome make possible – the greater cause that you are committed to and that inspires and excites you?
5   Are you still committed to the outcome?
6   If yes, then with respect to what's bothering you: what's really important about it?
7   And what can you do about it now? If the answer is nothing, when is a good time to reassess the issue?
8   What will you do about it immediately?
9   When will that be done?

This same coaching approach can be used by any two people where one acts as the coach first and then the roles are reversed.

Hot teams in action

Earlier in the chapter I asked you to do a little exercise aimed at building a motivating vision of what it would be like to create and lead a hot team. To give you a further insight, let me provide you with a description of the atmosphere and results achieved in one highly representative hot team: Steve Jobs and his initial team of four that created the Mac.

'The Mac team, headed by Apple (research) co-founder Steve Jobs, operated like a superstealth start-up within the company. Holed up in an ascetic, two-story building near a gas station dubbed the "Texaco Towers", the team was intensely competitive with other Apple divisions, such as the Lisa computer.

'Jobs set ridiculous deadlines: the caffeine-fuelled software team once debugged for 48 hours straight rather than face him without having finished the task ...

'Jobs' famous rebel yell – "It's better to be a pirate than join the Navy" – captured the renegade spirit that saw the team through 90-hour work weeks at stunningly low pay.

'In 1983, after three years of labour, the Mac was born. Priced at $2495, it featured a clean, intuitive graphic user interface that allowed non-programmers to use it almost instantly, without geek supervision. When it was turned on, a friendly little icon smiled out at the world. And the world smiled back – the Mac sold faster than any PC that came before.'

From Levenson, 'Six teams that changed the world', *Fortune*, 2006

Jobs applied the same principles in creating the iMac and the iPod almost two decades later.

Create a hot team in a couple of days

When your company is up and running and you feel ready, take the leadership team away for a couple of days and start to discuss the practices that you need to adopt to become a hot team. Almost all hot teams meet off-site for these sorts of meetings

rather than in their office. It seems to create the right sort of relaxed atmosphere.

You don't have to spend serious money on these two days.
You can meet at someone's house, go out for dinner and/or some
fun activity, and reconvene the following day.

Start by giving the speech that you produced in Chapter 8
about the company's purpose, ambitions and values. Do this
with more passion and conviction than ever before. Allow people to raise any questions and concerns. Acknowledge each concern as valid and if action is required, say what will be done
about it by when. Stay on the edge of reason – don't brush anything under the carpet but keep reminding people what you are
committed to.

Move on to a relationship meeting. Begin with the Gordon
Starr exercise I described earlier and then follow the three steps
for relationship meetings:

1 Acknowledge how much has been achieved so far.
2 Reinforce your priorities and strategy.
3 Let people say what's bothering them.

Take a break and then pick a problem that someone is currently
facing and run a breakdown meeting.

Pick an enemy – someone you will love to hate! Explore exactly why you hate them so much and how good it will feel to
beat them.

Finally decide what hot team practices you will adopt and
make a plan to incorporate them into your normal day-to-day
routine. Make sure someone is accountable for each action.

It's a good idea to repeat these leadership away-days every
quarter or so – you can run variations on the format of the day,
depending on current priorities and interests.

Remember to allow time for some fun.

Do something

Choose one or more of the hot team practices I have described and use it to address a real issue that you are facing at the moment, either in your current job, at home or in attempting to get your new company into action. For example:

- If you are working with a team at the moment, design and run a relationship meeting.
- If you are stuck on a problem, run a breakdown meeting.
- If you need some ideas, run a brainstorm.

Finally, pick an enemy for your new company right now – an organization you will love to hate, you are determined to destroy and that defines itself as everything you are not.

12

Powerful stuff: the principles in action

'He not busy being born is busy dying.'

Bob Dylan, 'It's Alright, Ma (I'm Only Bleeding)'

Dylan's lyrics are powerful stuff; in my opinion, none are more so than this profound example. When I use this quote in conferences, I almost always get delegates approaching me afterwards to say that it had a significant effect on them. I've even been told it might be the single most powerful thought in the universe. I'm not sure about that, but after all the interviews I've done and all the case studies I've examined while writing *Find Your Lighbulb*, I am positive that the principles I've given you are powerful enough to shift the odds decisively in your favour if you make the choice to get busy being born.

That was a decision I made for the fifth time in my life when I decided to come out of retirement and embark on a journey with my new company, Garlik. As I've mentioned before, Garlik provides individuals and their families with a means of controlling the way information about them is used in the digital world, as

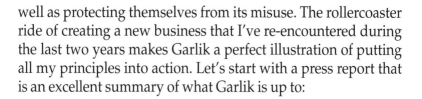
well as protecting themselves from its misuse. The rollercoaster ride of creating a new business that I've re-encountered during the last two years makes Garlik a perfect illustration of putting all my principles into action. Let's start with a press report that is an excellent summary of what Garlik is up to:

Government's loss is Garlik's gain

Launching a brand new data-privacy product to the media, days after the government managed to lose two discs containing the names, addresses and bank details of 25 million people, looked like a public relations masterstroke. In fact, it was simply good timing.

'Garlik, the online data protection company created by Egg founders Mike Harris and Tom Ilube, last night unveiled QDOS, a "digital status" tool that measures the online footprint of 45 million UK adults. Harris, who made his name at Firstdirect, selling direct banking to the masses, said the government's data transgression provided a timely backdrop to the launch. "This has been two years in the making," he said, "and then somebody did a very good job of raising awareness last week."

'Harris added that his intention was to build a global business out of QDOS, utilizing Garlik's "great knowledge and expertise in this sector." It was no empty pledge. Alongside Harris and Ilube, the Garlik team boasts a heavyweight line-up of technology and data experts, including Nigel Shadbolt, current president of the British Computer Society; Simon Davies, who founded privacy and data protection group Privacy International; and Sir Tim Berners-Lee, who, among other things, invented the Web.

'Shadbolt's contribution as Garlik's chief technology officer is key – as is that of Sir Tim, who is part of the start-up's advisory board – because QDOS runs on Semantic Web technology, which allows Garlik's database to locate and distinguish between

45 million UK adults, providing each with an individual digital-status score. Part of Professor Shadbolt's work at Southampton University involves the commercialization of Semantic Web technology.

'Why should we care about digital status? Garlik believes that as more and more of us start to organize our lives digitally, the value of our digital identities will become increasingly important. "With all the information available on the Internet," said Ilube, "in a couple of hours I would have enough to steal the identities of most of the people in this room."

'But despite the government's unwitting intervention last week, trying to scare consumers into understanding the power of their digital footprint is not working, he said. "We have given every adult in the UK a QDOS score and that's important because we want to drive engagement. We want to get millions of consumers engaging with their digital status, because when they do the conversation about digital identity will change suddenly and profoundly. This is your identity. This is who you are. It's not something to be afraid of."

'To acquire a QDOS rating, users simply type in their name and postcode. That information is checked against Garlik's huge, semantically tagged database, which then calculates your score, based on the extent of that person's online network, their popularity, their main online activity and how easy they are to find. The bigger the digital footprint, the bigger the score. Non-UK residents have been rated too, provided they are famous enough. The Dalai Lama has a rating of 5590, for example, while Bill Gates enjoys a slightly bigger score of 6402.

'The success of QDOS will depend greatly on how consumers value their score. Does a bigger footprint mean that your data is easier to steal? Is there information stored on long-forgotten sites that you'd rather wasn't there? Garlik's own research into the value of digital identity forms some interesting conclusions.

According to PCP Market Research, one in five adults have re-searched a prospective boss online before accepting a job, while 16% have used the Web to research prospective neighbours before completing a house purchase." The way you project yourself in the digital world really matters," said Ilube.

'So far Garlik has been pretty good at raising awareness – the World Economic Forum announced this afternoon that it had chosen the company as one of its technology pioneers for 2008 – but naturally one of the key questions for investors 3i and Doughty Hanson & Co. is whether or not Garlik can make any money out of it. Garlik's DataPatrol service, which claims to protect Web users from identity theft, requires a £3 monthly subscription, but Ilube offered little to suggest that in the short term QDOS will add anything more than goodwill to company coffers. "The key question at any venture capital pitch is, 'Yes, but how are you going to monetize their eyeballs?' I'm not sure I want my eyeballs monetized."

'Instead, he told *Director*, QDOS should be valued on its potential for future dominance of the sector. "Imagine if tens of millions of people worldwide got seriously engaged with their digital identities and there was only one company, Garlik, that was completely and unambiguously consumer-sided," he said. "I think there will be a whole range of products and services required in that industry to meet the consumer needs that emerge. But it's impossible to predict what those needs will be in advance."

'So no plans to profit from what would easily be the world's most accurate consumer database? "It may be, but we won't sell it," said Ilube. "We think there is more value in being possibly the world's only pure, consumer-sided identity company. There is more long-term value in that than any short-term value to be had from exploiting a database."

'QDOS is very much a work in progress – ultimately, the consumer reaction will shape how successful it becomes. But what

> Garlik has right now is an innovative product, marshalled by some of the greatest technical minds money can buy – led by a team with a proven track record in consumer marketing. HMRC's data slip might have been bad news for the government, but for data companies like Garlik, the future is looking increasingly profitable.'
>
> www.garlik.com
>
> From 'Government loss is Garlik's gain', *Director* magazine, 2007

Principles in action

1. Unleash your enthusiasm

In the early days, before anyone had invested a penny in Garlik, the idea lived only through Tom Ilube's enthusiasm. He was an evangelist for the idea of commercializing Semantic Web technology into something that could help organize people information on the Internet in a way that gave power to individuals. He didn't exactly stop people on the street, but it wasn't far off. Anybody who would listen got the full-on pitch. He didn't care if they weren't interested, he just moved on to the next person. Nobody listening to him was left in any doubt that he would do whatever it took to make his big idea happen.

Expressing enthusiasm is free of charge and available to all of us. If you express enthusiasm for your idea with passion and intensity, as Tom did, it will get amazing results.

I was so taken with his enthusiasm I didn't really listen to the details. My only question was – how big can this be? Once I was happy with that I took out my cheque book, invested and agreed to become Chairman.

2. Star in your own soap opera – create a Bold and Inspiring Future

When we started to think seriously about Garlik we began with the final chapter of our story, set a few years out. We said the following:

- The company we created has given individuals and their families real power in the use of their personal information in the digital world.
- For that to happen we had created a reality that didn't exist in 2005: everybody agrees that they have a digital identity, which is important and needs to be managed and protected.
- We have shifted power dramatically from those with the time, money and expertise to exploit people's information for their own ends to the individuals themselves.
- We are the good guys, the experts on the side of the individuals and their families. We fight against the bad guys who seek to abuse information.
- We achieved all of this through development and use of world class Semantic Web technology.

These statements are fixed: the enduring ends that we have chosen to always be committed to. Everything else we do is flexible – a means to an end.

We didn't set any specific financial targets, we just wanted to make it as big as possible. Setting a Bold and Inspiring Future goal is free of charge, easy and powerful. At Garlik it was the fundamental way we separated our ends and means – you will know by now how important that is. It keeps us focused on our ultimate destination. It means we do not become directionless even if we meet adverse circumstances. We always know that wherever we are today, the next steps we take are going to be in a direction that takes us closer towards our ultimate goal.

In addition, having our Bold and Inspiring Future written down is a continual reminder of why we are creating Garlik and what's important to us about the way we do it. It is a reminder that what we are doing is something we really care about and something that really matters to the world – that's a great motivator whenever the going gets tough.

3. Critics who count and Intelligent Insights

In order to produce a compelling business plan we spoke to everybody we thought might be able to tell us why our ideas wouldn't work. We spoke to technologists, marketing professionals, PR companies, banks and insurance companies. We spoke to venture capitalists; we spoke to entrepreneurs and lawyers. I'm sure we drove everybody crazy.

We ended up with two Intelligent Insights:

1   The state of the art on semantic technology was just not up to the job – we needed to use artificial intelligence to extract people information from the unstructured Web and then we needed to store it in a semantic database. The maximum size of these databases is measured in what are known as *triples*. You don't need to worry about what a triple is, but what you need to know is that people were quoting a limit of ten million triples and that we needed to get to a billion triples eventually (although 100 million or so would do initially). IBM alone were said to have invested zillions of pounds without cracking this problem.

2   Consumers were not interested in taking control of their digital identities – they didn't even know what it meant.

The only thing that could get consumers' attention was the problem of identity theft. Banks and insurance companies were successful in selling identity theft protection insurance based on people's growing fear of that problem. However, these products (as they were then) were criticized by consumer groups as being overpriced and offering no real protection. Even if you ignored that, the experts said you had to sell identity theft person-to-person to overcome people's objections and concerns. We were told that there was no way we could compete and that our technology was irrelevant to the problem anyway.

It was therefore obvious what our priorities should be: we needed to demonstrate that we could build a large scale semantic database and we needed to identify a product that used the technology and that we could sell competitively.

This led to the following statements of intent:

1   We will build a prototype clearly demonstrating our ability to use artificial intelligence to gather and collate people information for the digital world. We will store it in a semantic database, which is clearly capable of scaling beyond 100 million triples.
2   We will identify a product that offers genuine protection against identity theft and that uses our technology to differentiate it from the competition.

The big challenge at this stage was the technology prototype, where we needed to get breakthrough results. However, after a series of brainstorms and intense design meetings, we came up with an approach and produced a prototype capable of scaling to beyond 100 million triples – much to the critics' surprise. We also demonstrated an ability to use artificial intelligence to extract and collate people information in the digital world.

4. The art of customer insight

At Garlik, we started with a prototype – a demonstration of what we meant by digital identity. This was necessary because in talking about digital identity we were defining a new category, something that people had never really considered before – we had to show people, including ourselves, what a digital identity actually looked like. We had to understand what sort of emotions it provoked before we could start thinking about unmet needs.

Our prototype pulled together everything we could find out about an individual in the digital world and displayed it in a tabular form, as well as a graphically displayed network of relationships it had detected with companies and other people. The whole team used the product on themselves and we also asked about ten other people (friends, family, colleagues, business associates) to try it out. We nominated one member of our team to watch individuals using the product and ask them to describe how they were feeling about what they were seeing. How much insight was it giving them? How could it put them more in control of their information? Did it make the concept of a digital identity real and important for them?

The general reaction was almost always:

- 'Wow, that's powerful stuff – absolutely intriguing.'
- 'It's a bit scary – all that stuff out there about me? How would someone steal my identity using this?'
- 'How often does this change, I wonder – how often should I be looking at it?'
- 'I wonder what I should be doing about all of this information.'

Armed with these insights, we ran an idea-generation session (Chapter 4) that focused on ways in which we could use the technology to meet the apparently unmet emotional and functional needs that we had discovered. These included curiosity, a need to know if your identity is vulnerable or has already been stolen, and a need for advice and guidance.

We generated many product ideas to meet these needs before coming up with the one that seemed most promising to us. This was a product that continually patrolled the digital world for information about you, sending you a red alert if it found compromising or sensitive information and told you what to do about it.

We wrote an advert detailing the product and gathered reactions from the same people who had tried out the prototype. These reactions convinced us that we were on the right track, helping us to produce a compelling product pitch when we were seeking VC funding.

After we'd found funding, we used a professional market researcher to explore our product in much more detail using about 50 people – some in groups of eight, some in one-to-one interviews. This process delivered detailed feedback on what worked, what didn't and why, what sort of people seemed most interested in the product, and the price people would be prepared to pay. This enabled us to fine-tune the design and the marketing.

We continued with low-cost professional customer research (each round only involving about eight customers) all the way through to launch. This allowed us to continue to refine the product design using a series of prototypes and pilots.

5. Produce a financial plan and get your business funded

We funded Garlik using the *growth route*. We funded the development of the initial concept ourselves; then, with an initial business plan and pitch, we brought in five angel investors at £20,000 each to complete the prototype. We just asked everybody we knew if they were interested in investing or knew someone who was. It's amazing how often this works.

When we were ready for further investment, we approached a number of VCs using our own contacts and those of our angel investors, who proved very useful. We produced a heavyweight business plan and pitch (exactly as I described in Chapter 5) and we raised £3m from 3i and Doughty Hanson.

6. Know your ends from your means

The first thing we did once funding was no longer a concern was to produce a dynamic business plan:

- We wanted to define a set of interim ends (a year ahead) that would be the first step towards our ultimate goal.
- We wanted to allocate our resources in order to achieve those ends.
- We wanted to allocate a single accountability for the achievement of each end.
- We wanted to give ourselves something that we could use to monitor our progress during the year.
- We wanted to know what was fixed (the ends) so that we could amend the means we were using to achieve the ends throughout the year if necessary.

You will see the exact plan that we came up with reproduced in full in Chapter 6. We used this plan throughout the year to keep on track to our interim goals (i.e. what we had said we would achieve by the end of 2006). We amended our detailed approach (the means) many times, but never lost track of the fixed goals (ends) that we had set for ourselves.

There are of course countless examples of ways in which we changed our means without affecting our end. In the final few weeks before our launch, for instance, we produced a series of prototypes and pilots. In each case we got feedback from potential customers that allowed us to refine the design based on what we were learning. We kept researching with consumers and experts to be sure we were meeting real unmet rational and emotional needs.

As a consequence of this we dropped the advice and insurance feature, as well as some of the information exploration tools within the original product design: they added considerably to the price and hardly contributed to either the functional or emotional needs we were addressing. On the other hand, we added a monthly risk assessment and a regular monitoring of credit reports that were not in the original design but both added value. In doing this we stayed committed to the end that we had set ourselves: a product that provided a unique form of protection against identity theft.

It's a pretty easy process to put an action plan together in the way I'm recommending. We only spent a couple of days on it and we didn't use any external specialist expertise.

7. Embrace brand, reputation, publicity and promotion

At Garlik we used professional help on this matter but of course you can do it yourself. If you choose to do so you will be in good company – Google, eBay and Apple all did this in the early days, so don't be put off. Remember, when you design a brand you start with a central idea, a promise and a set of values.

The central idea of Garlik was to illuminate the digital world. Our brand promise was to provide powerful insight and our core value was the fact that we are the good guys protecting you from the bad guys. All these premises have had enduring power for us. They have shaped pretty much every action we have ever taken. We never forget that our job is to deliver that promise of powerful insight and, in doing so, we maintain that we are the good guys.

We based our promotion of Garlik around a campaign developed for us by the PR company Band and Brown. The initial release was headed: 'Organized crime targets broadband Britain.'

The heart of the story was this:

> 'There's a new wave of ID theft hitting Britain, from which firewalls and virus-checkers offer no protection. Organized gangs are collating personal data about us in a matter of hours and using it to manufacture stolen identities which they sell on for criminal misuse – illegal immigration, fraud, even terrorism. Garlik is a new organization set up to help people take control of their identity. Today we're launching DataPatrol as the most effective way of avoiding becoming a victim of identity theft.'

It was effective. It secured us significant press and TV coverage, which, supplemented by a simple digital marketing campaign, scored us 60,000 customers for our initial pilot product.

8. Culture is critical

The job of creating a culture in order to deliver the brand promise is largely a matter of continually communicating what you believe in, what you are doing and why.

You will have already read the powerful speech with which Tom established the culture at Garlik (Chapter 8). This was designed to educate people about our company and our brand, show them what role they could play to make a real difference, explain how our brand values show up in the organization, and illustrate examples of behaviours that would support the brand and those that would not be tolerated.

Tom communicated the thoughts in this speech incessantly, at every opportunity, in the early days of Garlik. The first time I heard it was in December 2005. We were just about to bank the cheque from the VCs and the whole extended team who had been working on Garlik had gathered for a celebration. The reaction was immediate – we all realized that we were aligned towards a Bold and Inspiring Future and the behaviours that would facilitate this. There was no room for doubt.

Tom continued to communicate in the same way almost every day thereafter. After Garlik launched, he was able to express the same thoughts in press interviews. After a while for everybody inside and outside the company, it just became the way things were at Garlik.

We recruited people who shared our values and commitment. I can't remember a single occasion where either Tom or I had to stamp out anything that wasn't in line with what we wanted from the brand or the culture. Garlik is definitely a nice place to work and we definitely have fun. If you pay enough attention to your culture early on, that's the prize – you get what you want from people and they get what they want as well.

9. The principles of leadership

When it comes to leadership, your key tool is to create a power gap. This is the gap between what you are committed to achieving in the future and your totally honest and rational assessment of the way things are today.

To create a power gap you must:

1   Accurately describe the current status of things, neither letting anyone get too gloomy about it, nor letting anyone get away with spin (i.e. sexing up the current situation to show themselves or the current situation an unreasonably good light).

'We've got 60,000 customers. We have thoroughly researched their perception of DataPatrol as a product and we've also looked again at our target consumer's attitudes to identity protection and management products. We drew a few conclusions from that research:

'A significant number of consumers are more likely to buy identity theft products from people they already had a relationship with (banks, telecom companies, ISPs etc) than a new company like Garlik

'Apart from identity theft, the whole topic of digital identity is poorly understood.

'DataPatrol is liked by some customers but there is a lot we could do it make it more relevant, useful and engaging for others.'

Tom Ilube, January 2007 – his words to Garlik and its shareholders

---

2   You must always acknowledge the effort and commitment and indeed the real achievement behind what has been achieved so far.

'We have established ourselves as a powerful new voice in the arena of digital identity. Our technology is a world leader and we have 60,000 people engaged with our first product. These are significant achievements and demonstrate the skill and commitment of everyone who has worked for us. We are extremely well placed to move forward from here.'

Tom Ilube, January 2007

---

3   You must continue to express total faith that you will achieve your Bold and Inspiring Future.

'I want there to be no doubt where we are headed. We are already punching above our weight. Everyone who matters in this world of digital identity wants to talk to us and we can and will go on to build a powerful and valuable company that has a major impact globally. We will give individuals and their families more power over use of their information in the digital world.'

Tom Ilube, January 2007

---

4   You need to focus people's attention on what matters next.

'In 2007 we will produce a new product called DataPatrol Advanced that takes account of what people have told us about the current product. We will sell this product direct to consumers.

'We will develop a number of distribution partnerships with (for example) banks so that other companies can sell DataPatrol Advanced for us.

'We will design and implement a mass-market consumer product that will attract millions of visitors from the US and the UK to our site and demonstrate in a graphic and engaging way the importance of digital identity.

'We will produce a business plan for 2007–9 and use that plan to raise an extra £6m of funding to take us forward.

*'We will achieve all of these things and we will take a further
giant step towards our ultimate goal.'*

Tom Ilube, January 2007

---

10. Smart risks

At Garlik, every step we took towards our Big and Inspiring Future goal was carefully chosen and well thought through. Every choice we took and every optional investment we made met the smart risks criteria.

The biggest risk we took was putting our own money in Garlik before we knew the technology could be made to work. No VC would have taken that risk, but it was a smart risk for us:

- We were crystal clear about what we were taking on.
- The potential upside was worth the personal and financial investment.
- We would back ourselves to pull this off more than five times out of ten.
- We knew what we would we have to believe to think this would be successful – and we did believe those things.
- We could afford to fail at this, financially and from a reputation point of view.

The development and launch of QDOS is the biggest step into the unknown we have taken. QDOS is a number – we all have one – it's a measure of our status in the digital space. By calculating hundreds of millions of QDOS scores and inviting people to engage, explore and take control of their own score, we believe we have a way of popularizing the conversation about digital identity, taking a huge leap forward in our ambitions.

We have no idea how to make money out of it yet, but it's a smart risk because:

- we are crystal clear about what we are taking on
- the potential upside is huge compared to a very modest investment
- we totally back ourselves to find a way to make money out of it eventually
- we believe it will be successful
- we can afford to fail and move on.

11. Create and maintain a hot team

Garlik started with a hot team – one with powerful and talented individuals who all shared a powerful vision. We have kept our team hot by maintaining context and engaging in some specific team practices.

Maintaining context is about giving meaning to events so people don't make up what they might mean. During 2007 we tried a new approach to digital marketing using a top advertising agency (and a lot more money) on the design of the display ads, on media buying, and on the copy in the emails we sent out to our customers. It didn't work as well as we had expected.

The natural reaction of people was to wonder what was wrong – is it the brand, the product, the agency or us? The gloom soon spreads and the team goes off the boil. A rapid piece of communication in such circumstances soon gets the team fired up again. I was coaching the marketing team when this happened. This is what I told them:

'Well we know something else that doesn't work now, don't we. Let's focus on what is working. Our PR campaigns are working, our search campaigns are working. I'm excited about the distribution deals coming through and QDOS is a game changer. Next year we will have hundreds of millions of people able to engage with their digital identity and all from nothing just 12 months ago. That's the biggest step we have yet taken towards our future. OK, there's a lot to do in the next few weeks – let's go!'

In addition, the specific practices of hot teams I described in Chapter 11 are of course in common and regular use throughout the company. As well as defining a clear enemy, we also regularly engage in meetings to give feedback on product designs, promotional activities and major decisions, relationship meetings, one-to-one meetings, brainstorm meetings, and (thankfully) only the occasional breakdown meeting.

These various types of meetings are all a way of life at Garlik. Meetings get a bad press because they are often poorly executed; done properly, they are a great way to reinforce commitment to the company and to each other and to have some fun.

Garlik's future

As with any new business, there are never any guarantees – we can't see into the future. But there is no doubt that Garlik has done very well so far. It is a perfect example of how you can create something substantial and worthwhile out of nothing more than an idea. Garlik has definitely established itself as a serious player, but it's still too early to say just how successful it will be. If you are interested in following the story as Garlik develops further, then visit me on my website (www.findyourlightbulb.com) and read about any new insights I discover as a result.

The final word

This should definitely go to the man who inspired the title of this book: Thomas Edison. Many people say that the modern world was effectively created by Edison's inventions, the most famous of which was the lightbulb – declared impossible by experts at the time, of course.

> *'Genius is one per cent inspiration and ninety-nine per cent perspiration. Accordingly, a "genius" is often merely a talented person who has done all of his or her homework.'*

I firmly believe that a willingness to 'do homework' and learn from others is the key to success. I have made that thought the watchword of my own career – my own approach has been to learn from others, find what works and then improve it.

My intention has been to give you access to everything I have learnt over the last 20 years in a way that you can put into practice immediately. All that's left is for you to decide whether to harness the power you were born with – the power to unleash a new idea and change the world forever.

And on that thought, I'll leave you to make up your own mind about what you do next.

I wish you luck and good fortune, whatever that may be.

Bibliography

Bennis, Warren (1997) 'The secret of great groups', *Leader to Leader*, no. 3, pp. 29–33.

Bennis, Warren (1997) *Organizing Genius*, Nicola Brearley Publishing.

Bilimoria, Karan (2007) *Bottled for Business: The Less Gassy Guide to Entrepreneurship*, Capstone.

Branson, Richard (1998) *Losing My Virginity*, Random House.

Branson, Richard (2007) *Screw It – Let's Do It*, Virgin Books.

Buckland, William, Hatcher, Andrew and Birkinshaw, Julian (2003) *Inventuring: Why Big Companies Must Think Small*, McGraw-Hill Professional.

Cohen, Adam (2002) *The Perfect Store*, Little, Brown.

Collins, James C. and Porras, Jerry J. (1998) *Built to Last*, Century.

Collins, Jim (2001) *Good to Great*, Random House Business Books.

Dennis, Felix (2006) *How to Get Rich*, Ebury Press.

Dourado, Phil and Blackburn, Dr. Phil (2005) *Seven Secrets of Inspired Leaders*, Capstone.

Goss, Tracy (1996) *The Last Word on Power*, Doubleday.

Grossman, Lev (2005) 'How Apple does it', *Time*, no. 17, 24 October.

Hennesy, Peter (2001) *The Prime Minister: The Office and its Holders Since 1945*, Penguin Books.

Kelley, Tom (1995) *The Art of Innovation: Lessons in Creativity by Ideo*, Doubleday.

Kranz, Gene (2000) *Failure is Not an Option: Mission Control from Mercury to Apollo 13 and Beyond*, Simon and Schuster.

Levenson, Eugenia (2006) 'Six teams that changed the world', *Fortune*, 31 May.

Lovell, Jim and Kluger, Jeffrey (1994) *Apollo 13*, Houghton Mifflin.

Murray, W.H. (1951) *The Scottish Himalayan Expedition*, Dent.

Sodowick, Adam and Watts, Jenny (2005) *Exceptional Entrepreneurship, Adapted From the Fifty Lessons Management Collection*, BBC Books.

Unknown (2007) 'Government loss is Garlik's gain', *Director*, November.

Utterback, James, M. (1994) *Mastering the Dynamics of Innovation*, Harvard Business School Press.

Vise, David A. and Malseed, Mark (2005) *The Google Story*, Bantam Dell.

Walker, Rob (2003) 'The guts of a new machine', *New York Times*, 30 November.

Young, Jeffrey S. (2006) *iCon Steve Jobs: The Greatest Second Act in the History of Business*, John Wiley & Sons.

Index

Midland Bank (now HSBC) 8, 10, 61,
    73, 132–3, 201–202, 205
mindset 17–19
MoniLink 12
Moritz, Michael 214
Mother advertising agency 12, 24
motivation 28–33
Murray, Jamie 42
Murray, W.H. 84
My Family Care 64–5

National Health Service (NHS) 179
needs
    functional and emotional 59–60
    Maslow's hierarchy 54
    unmet 68–70
Newcomb, Simon 45
NeXt 158
Nokia 39, 160
Northern Rock 139

Ocado 92
Olympic Games 20
One2One 43
Oracle 63
Orange 140, 141, 142

Pacific Gas and Electric (PG&E) 123,
    180–81
Packard, Dave 156
Page, Larry 68, 157, 214
partnerships 147–8
passion 58–9
patents 79
Pauling, Linus 53
planning see business plan; dynamic
    action planning; financial plan
Pole, Seb 11, 12–13
Porras, Jerry 26

Power Gap
    brainstorming 188
    condition of satisfaction 106
    create hot leadership team 194–7
    creating 184–7
    prepare for competition 189–91
    principles in action 187–97
    take risks with care 193–4
    watch the cash 192–3
power of the gods 16
principles
    art of customer insight 243–4
    create Bold and Inspiring Future
        240–41
    create/maintain hot team 252–3
    critics who count 241–2
    culture is critical 247–8
    embrace brand, reputation,
        publicity, promotion 246–7
    enthusiasm 239
    get business funded 244–5
    intelligent insights 241–2
    know ends from means 245–6
    principles of leadership 248–51
    produce financial plan 244–5
    smart risks 251–2
    star in own soap opera 240–41
problem solving 223–6
Prudential 18–19, 32, 96, 151–2, 177,
    207, 211
public relations (PR) 145, 223
publicity 133, 246–7
Pukka Herbs 11, 12–13, 154

QDOS 251, 253

Racal 96
Raddice, Vittorio 23
rallying the troops speech 168–9